D0427132

OVERLOOK ILLUSTRATED LIVES:

Samuel Beckett

Gerry Dukes lectures in literature at Mary
Immaculate College, University of Limerick.
With the actor Barry McGovern he selected
the texts from Beckett's post-war
trilogy of novels to make *I'll go on*, which has
played around the world. He has published
essays, reviews and articles on modern Irish
writing and visual art in Europe and the
United States. *First Love and Other Novellas*, his
annotated edition of Beckett's novellas, was
published in 2000. He currently lives in
Dublin.

Samuel Beckett

Gerry Dukes

THE OVERLOOK PRESS
WOODSTOCK & NEW YORK

First published in the United States in 2002 by
The Overlook Press, Peter Mayer Publishers, Inc.
Woodstock & New York

WOODSTOCK:
One Overlook Drive
Woodstock, NY 12498
www.overlookpress.com
[For individual orders, bulk and special sales, contact our Woodstock office]

NEW YORK:
141 Wooster Street
New York, NY 10012

Published by arrangement with Penguin Books Ltd.

A CIP record for this book is available from the Library of Congress

Printed and bound in Great Britain by The Bath Press

9 8 7 6 5 4 3 2 1
ISBN 1-58567-266-1

Contents

'But tell me the story of your life, then we'll see. My life! I cried. Why yes, he said, you know, that kind of – what shall I say? He brooded for a time, no doubt trying to think of what life could well be said to be a kind. In the end he went on, testily, Come now, everyone knows that. He jogged me in the ribs. No details, he said, the main drift, the main drift. But as I remained silent he said, Shall I tell you mine, then you'll see what I mean. The account he then gave was brief and dense, facts, without comment. That's what I call a life, he said, do you follow me now?'

Samuel Beckett, *The Calmative*

The producer of a book such as this incurs many debts. My first one is to Caroline Pretty of Penguin, who commissioned it and who refused to panic as the deadlines came and went with metronomic regularity. Pernilla Pearce, the picture editor, possesses and deployed sleuthing skills that should be the envy of any researcher. Sarah Coward copy-edited the final version and effected an improvement with every intervention. Edward Beckett and Caroline Murphy (née Beckett) have been, as always, most generous and helpful in all matters relating to their uncle and his estate. Anyone who undertakes even a modest biographical essay on Beckett owes a great deal to the three major biographies that have already appeared and I freely acknowledge debts to Deirdre Bair, Anthony Cronin and Professor James Knowlson – their books are individually listed in the Bibliography. For leads to rich photographic sources I thank Walter Asmus, Ruby Cohn, Marek Kedzierski and Lutfi Özkök. For helpful materials, hints, guesses and suggestions I thank Bruce Arnold, David Davison (and the Irish Picture Library), Phyllis Gaffney, Terence Killeen, Barry McGovern, John Minihan, Sean Ó Mórdha and Eoin O'Brien. I am particularly grateful to the Joyce Estate for permission to publish a transcription of a postcard sent by Joyce to Beckett's brother, Frank, in 1938.

Work on this book was greatly facilitated by the granting of leave of absence from teaching by An Fo-choiste Stiúrtha of An Bórd Rialaithe at Mary Immaculate College, University of Limerick, for which I am most grateful. Linda Ashton and the staff at the Harry Ransom Humanities Resource Center of the University of Texas at Austin were professionally helpful and personally charming, as were Mike Bott and the staff at the Beckett International Foundation Archive at the University of Reading. I hereby warn them all that I shall be back soon to impose on them again. Finally, I must thank Bríd, who added rescue from error to all the other obligations I owe her. Errors that remain are exclusively mine.

Gerry Dukes, Dublin, 2001

SAMUEL BECKETT

1

At the time of his death in his eighty-fourth year, just before Christmas in 1989, Samuel Beckett had over sixty years of match-less creativity to his credit. He had written, in two languages – English and French – criticism and poetry, prose fiction and drama, a film and nearly two dozen plays for radio and television. He was in his late forties before the worth and importance of his work were generally recognized and by then he had not the slightest interest in celebrity, believing that it was the writing rather than the writer that should be the main focus of attention. Hence he granted very few interviews to journalists. Nevertheless, he made himself avail-able to many critics and scholars interested in his work, with whom he could be quite forthcoming, tolerant and helpful.

Many universities and academic institutions sought to confer honorary degrees upon him but he declined all except a Doctorate in Letters from his Alma Mater in Dublin in 1959. Ten years later he accepted the Nobel Prize for Literature but declined attending the ceremony, delegating his French publisher to accept the prize on his behalf. His wife regarded the award as a 'catastrophe' because it inevitably meant that atten-tion was paid to his person rather than to his work.

Left Beckett signing limited editions of his work in 1977.
Overleaf Beckett and his wife, Suzanne, at Père Lachaise in Paris in January 1984 after the cremation of Roger Blin, the first director of Waiting for Godot.

Beckett was shy of publicity and wary of speaking in public although he was not camera-shy, as is amply evidenced in the following pages. The bulk of the photographs arise from his work in the theatre, where he often felt at ease with his fellow artists. Included also are some more informal family 'snaps' and a selec-tion of formal portraits by some of the leading photographers of

Beckett with a very young relative.

the time. In many of these Beckett is revealed as strikingly photo-
genic and open.

   Meeting him was always a pleasure because of his clockwork
punctuality and his extraordinary warmth, courtesy and generosity.
A letter from him (or rather a postcard) was a provocation to deci-
pherment, a teasing puzzle the solution to which could take hours.
But poring over Beckett's words, whether handwritten or printed,
or listening to them in a theatre, is likely to be as rewarding and
disquieting an experience as one can have, because his words con-
nect directly with what it is to 'be'.

2

Throughout his life Samuel Beckett maintained that he had been born on Good Friday, 13 April 1906. He had his family's assurance on this matter – particularly his mother's – but he was bedevilled by the fact that his official birth certificate records 13 May as his birthday. The official record is in error; the registry clerk simply entered the wrong month on the certificate, as is evidenced by the birth announcement in the *Irish Times* published on 16 April 1906. The error was compounded when Beckett applied for his first passport, as a passport application must be supported by an official birth certificate, and subsequent renewals take the essential details from the expired or expiring one.

The Huguenot Becketts came to Ireland in the eighteenth century, fleeing religious persecution in France where they were members of an oppressed minority. Refugee Huguenots had been arriving in Ireland since the middle of the previous century, attracted to settle by various incentive schemes designed to promote the pacification of the indigenous Irish and the colonization of the territory of Ireland. They were an industrious people, bringing with them

The announcement of Beckett's birth in the Irish Times, *16 April 1906; conclusive evidence that his birth certificate and passport were both in error. Note the typographical error in the announcement – it lacks a final period.*

BIRTHS.

BECKETT—April 13th, at Cooldrinagh, Foxrock, the wife of W. F. Beckett, of a son

MACNAMARA—April 12th, at Mountmellick, the wife of J. Macnamara, of a daughter.

RUDD—On Easter Sunday, April 15th, at 60 Rathgar road, the wife of the Rev. T. E. Rudd, Rector of Castleblayney, of a daughter.

SIMPSON—April 13th, at 3 Rosmeen Gardens, Kingstown, the wife of George Simpson, of a daughter.

their skills in glass-making, goldsmithying and textile-weaving. Samuel Beckett's direct ancestors on his paternal side were notable poplin-makers who, by the beginning of the nineteenth century, had already begun to diversify into building and architecture. Beckett's father, William (1871–1933), became a successful quantity surveyor, though his given occupation on Samuel Beckett's birth certificate is 'Civil Engineer'. So successful was he that he built a substantial house in the fashionable south County Dublin suburb of Foxrock into which he moved with his young, pregnant wife, May, in 1902.

It was in this house, named Cooldrinagh after the family home of May Beckett (née Roe, 1871–1950), that the couple's two sons were born: Francis in 1902 and Samuel in 1906.

Beckett's mother's people had come to Ireland in Cromwellian times and had become landowners in the south midlands. Samuel Roe, Beckett's maternal

Left William Beckett, successful *quantity surveyor, sportsman and solid citizen.*

Below Cooldrinagh, the Beckett *family home in Foxrock, named after Beckett's mother's family home in County Kildare. The name is an Anglicization of a Gaelic phrase meaning 'behind the blackthorn'.*

Previous page *The bow window of the room in which Beckett was born on Good Friday, 1906.*

grandfather, was both a landowner with tenantry and in business as a grain merchant and miller in north County Kildare and had a large house – Cooldrinagh – on extensive grounds in Leixlip in that county. He died relatively young and at a time when his fortunes were in decline. An indication of that decline is the fact that May, who was only fifteen years old at the time of his death, joined the staff of the Adelaide Hospital in Dublin as a nurse. It was at this hospital that she first encountered William Beckett who was being treated there for a bout of pneumonia.

In 1902, when William and May Beckett established themselves at the newly built Cooldrinagh, Foxrock was a tastefully developing suburb not far from the sea and close to the foothills of the Dublin and Wicklow Mountains. The main arterial road to the south-east ran through Cornelscourt, the adjacent village, and Foxrock was also served by a suburban rail line, which ran from Dublin City to the seaside resort of Bray, where it joined the main line to the south-east. These amenities were merely a few minutes' walk from Cooldrinagh, as was Tullow Church, where the family attended worship. Carrickmines Golf Club, where Beckett was to spend a considerable amount of time in his youth and early adult years, was within easy walking distance and Cooldrinagh itself had both a croquet lawn and a tennis court. This was the tranquil setting for Beckett's life until he went to boarding-school at the age of fourteen.

Foxrock may have been tranquil during Beckett's infancy and childhood but Ireland in general, and Dublin in particular, were not. The city had lost its status as a legislative capital when Ireland became an integral part of the United Kingdom of Great Britain and Ireland with the passing of the Act of Union in 1800. Following the Union, the Penal Laws, which were a debilitating feature of the Williamite Settlement of the late 1690s (that is, debilitating to the majority Roman Catholic population) and which underpinned the so-called Protestant Ascendancy, were gradually dismantled. Catholic emancipation was finally achieved in 1829; the Church of Ireland was disestablished in the 1860s; educational provision for Catholics was slowly expanded; and access to the so-called professions was opened up. These and other social and legislative changes accelerated the formation of a Catholic middle class. In practical terms, however, there were two middle classes separated by confessional allegiance: Protestant and Catholic. This separation was reflected in the provision of schools and colleges, sporting organizations and hospitals, and in patterns of employment. Social interaction between the two classes tended to be minimal. In fact, just before Beckett's father, William, met his future wife, he had courted the daughter of William Martin Murphy (a leading Catholic capitalist, newspaper proprietor and prime mover of the infamous Dublin Lockout of 1913) but had encountered resistance to the proposed marriage from both families and his plans had foundered.

A social context characterized by such sectarian division inevitably gave rise to values and patterns of behaviour that may be described as hypocritical, in so far as public appearance did not necessarily conform to private realities. A commitment to outward display of control and normality belied inner tensions and alienation. Beckett was to suffer the damaging psychological effects of such hypocrisy and subsequently to exploit it relentlessly in his work once he had come to terms with it. His character Molloy complains:

> And if I have always behaved like a pig, the fault lies not with me but with my superiors, who corrected me only on points of detail instead of showing me the essence of the system, after the manner of the great English schools, and the guiding principles of good manners, and how to proceed, without going wrong, from the former to the latter, and how to trace back to its ultimate source a given comportment. For that would have allowed me, before parading in public certain habits such as the finger in the nose, the scratching of the balls, digital emunction and the peripatetic piss, to refer them to the first rules of a reasoned theory.

Such disjunction between socially validated modes of behaviour and individual practice, between the acceptable and the necessary, was to generate in Beckett's work some of his most piercingly tragic and scabrously comic effects.

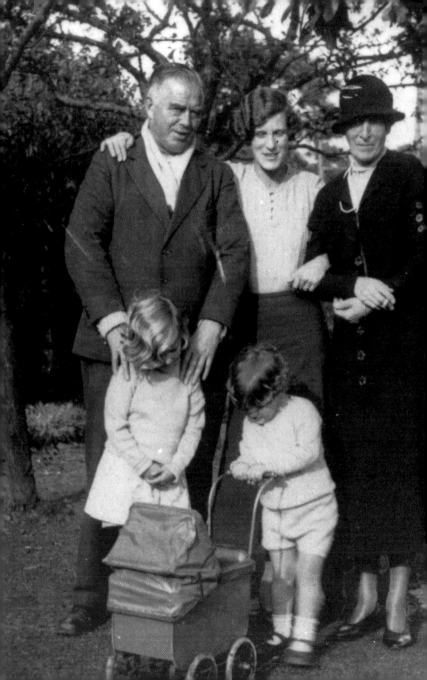

Bill and May Beckett with their niece Sheila Page (née Roe) and her children. Sheila and her sister, Molly, had spent many holidays with Beckett's family and he was greatly attached to his cousins.

Beckett with his cousin Molly Roe.

Life at Cooldrinagh during Beckett's early years must have been pleasant and comfortable, at least to the outside observer. As the Beckett boys grew up they inherited from their father a love of sport of many sorts. They had croquet and tennis at home, swimming a short bicycle ride away and, as they went through the same schools, cricket, rugby football and boxing. And when they were old enough to wield the clubs, golf was taken up too. But there were non-athletic pursuits also: the boys collected stamps and played chess together – a pastime that became almost a passion for Beckett. Some years before his death, when his country house at Ussy was broken into and various items stolen, the loss he

regretted most was that of a chess set
he had inherited from one of his uncles
who had coached him in the game. It
was one of the very few items he had retained from his childhood.

Beckett with his cousin Sheila Page in the summer of 1961.

A major modification to family life at Cooldrinagh occurred
in 1913 when Beckett's mother's brother, Edward Roe, became a
widower. He was then working in Nyasaland (now Malawi) and
he arranged for his children – a son and two daughters – to attend
boarding-schools in Dublin. The two girls, Sheila and Molly Roe,
spent all their school holidays with the Becketts in Foxrock until
their father remarried and was reunited with his children in Britain
after the First World War. Beckett formed an affectionate attachment

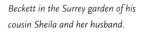

Beckett in the Surrey garden of his cousin Sheila and her husband.

to his two female cousins, who were a few years older than he; an attachment that continued long into the future.

The brothers' first schooling took place at a kindergarten run by the Elsner sisters in Leopardstown, a few minutes' walk from Cooldrinagh. It was in this establishment that Beckett first learned music – specifically the piano – and he was to take private piano lessons for quite a number of years, eventually becoming a proficient player. In fact music and piano-playing became for Beckett a lifelong refuge and relaxation. Beckett was bright and intelligent and learned to read at the Elsner kindergarten. For a boy who participated so fully in sports he was unusually given to reading. He read voraciously until his early adulthood when his serious reading became ancillary to his writing. He was given to 'light reading' all through his life – thrillers and the like – but he never lost what has been described as his *boulimie de savoir*, his keen appetite for knowledge.

When he was nine years old Beckett followed his brother, Frank, into Earlsfort House, a private school in the city a few hundred yards from the Harcourt Street terminus of the rail line that ran through Foxrock, the Dublin and South Eastern Railway (known colloquially as the 'Slow and Easy'). When Frank moved to Portora Royal School in County Fermanagh as a boarder, the younger Beckett continued for another three years to commute by train into Dublin every schoolday. Memories of those journeys and that railway were to prove tenacious, surfacing in many of his works written years later: in prose from *Watt* to *Textes pour rien*; and in drama from *All That Fall* to *That Time*. In late April and early May 1916 his regular commuting was interrupted when the train service was suspended during the Easter Rising in Dublin. In putting down the Rising the British Army had recourse to the use of artillery and widespread damage was caused to the city centre: even the *Irish Times* had to suspend publication. Indirect and ironic reference to the Rising is made in chapter four of his novel *Murphy*: the only direct reference is in the first chapter of *Mercier and Camier*, where the narrator mentions 'the domestic skirmish' that took place during 'the great upheaval' of the First World War. Ten-year-old Beckett was taken one evening to the foothills to see the burning city to the north, and some sixty years later he remembered the event with horror. In fact, from 1916 until the summer of 1923, when the civil war that followed the Anglo-Irish War (the so-called 'Troubles') ended, the political and security situation in Ireland was dangerous when it was not lethal. Beckett's formative years were spent in a country at war.

It would be a mistake, however, to imagine that Ireland was afflicted by a general conflagration. The Anglo-Irish war (1919–21) was fought mainly in the countryside, as was the subsequent civil war. The impact of the 'Troubles' on Dublin City and environs was not great but it is worth mentioning that the 'Slow and Easy' suffered disruption by twenty-three separate hold-ups carried out by Republican irregulars and criminals during the course of the civil war. Other railway journeys provided young Beckett with novel experiences. When he returned to Portora (where he was enrolled in 1920) after the summer vacation in September 1921, he discovered that the school was now located in a new country, anomalously named Northern Ireland. Late the following year, making the reverse journey home, he found that his native city was now located in the Irish Free State.

Beckett's career at Portora was notable not for his academic but for his athletic successes. He excelled at swimming, boxing, rugby and cricket; in fact, in his final year at the school he was captain of the senior cricket team, an efficient bowler and a steady batsman. He formed friendships at Portora that endured long into the future, the most abiding one being with Geoffrey Thompson, who was to be helpful and dependable until his death in 1976.

Having completed his secondary schooling at Portora, Beckett simply followed the standard path for Portorans and entered into Trinity College in Dublin. His brother, Frank, was already there studying civil engineering (he would in due course enter his father's firm). With the continuity of the Beckett family profession apparently secured, the younger son did not feel any pressure to study for a professional qualification. His school grades had been good so he registered as a student of Arts; of Modern Languages in particular. His choice was to prove crucial because his studies in French and Italian brought him into contact with and to the notice

Right Young Beckett with the Portora junior cricket team during his second year at the school in 1921.
Below Beckett with the senior boys' rugby team at Portora in 1923.

of two professors: Thomas Rudmose-Brown and Walter Starkie. Rudmose-Brown was unusual for a university professor in that not only was he a scholar of classical French literature but he also had a lively and professional interest in contemporary French literature, as a critic and anthology-compiler. In addition he possessed the ability to communicate his enthusiasm and interest in contemporary literature to his students. From Starkie, Beckett acquired an initial interest in Italian literature. Beckett quickly developed an abiding interest in the work of Dante, an interest that was to be formative for his own literary productions throughout his life.

The transformation of Samuel Beckett from schoolboy athlete to star student was gradual – early on he suffered the indignity of a tutor's reprimand for not 'keeping terms' – that is, not attending the required classes. He maintained his commitment to cricket, playing for the Trinity first eleven. And he became an avid motorcyclist. But by the end of his third year at Trinity his grades had improved spectacularly, so much so that he gained a Foundation Scholarship, which entitled him to rooms in the college, reduced fees and a small emolument each term. His academic success opened up for him the prospect of moving out of home and gaining a small but important degree of independence. (Full independence from his family, however, was not achieved until twenty-five years later, in the first half of the 1950s, when the earnings from his writing became sufficient for his needs.)

Leaving home was probably not a huge wrench for Beckett: he had become used to being away from home, having been a boarder at Portora. Additionally, his relationship with his parents was entering a new phase. Life at Cooldrinagh was unostentatiously comfortable, with domestic help and a gardener and, of course, loving and indulgent parents. William Beckett was a prosperous provider and Beckett, as a young child, had an uncomplicated relationship with his father with whom he shared many interests, particularly his love of sports. As his academic interests deepened, however, this relationship inevitably underwent changes. Beckett was aware it was he who was changing – in a four-line poem, 'Gnome', written and published in 1934, the

Facing page May Beckett in *the embrasure of a window at* Cooldrinagh.

year following his father's death, he refers to 'the loutishness of learning' from which the world politely turns. He would return to this reflective note of self-criticism in his own final years in brief letters to Mary Manning – a friend from his youth – where he regrets not having taken his father's advice to go for a clerkship in Guinness's brewery when he left Portora.

The qualitative change in his relationship with his mother was more aggravated. May Beckett had brought her boys up to be well behaved, courteous and mannerly. She was strict, perhaps even severe, in matters of decorum and formality and could be harsh in her response to what she thought were lapses. To such a woman spontaneity and boisterousness were deplorable because they betokened a lack of control, the absence of a proper commitment to a narrowly defined notion of respectability. Her son Frank conformed to her expectations, qualified as a civil engineer, gained experience in India and came home to join his father's firm. Samuel, however, not only would not conform but, increasingly, could not. His relationship with his mother was to become stormy and fraught and generate much unhappiness for both of them. Yet he was always aware that he became what her 'savage loving' (his phrase) had made of him.

The fact that Beckett was in his third year at Trinity before his grades moved into the top rank suggests that he may have had some difficulty in adapting to university life. In Portora his athletic accomplishments conferred on him a prominence and popularity within the relatively small community of the school. Trinity was a much larger institution and Beckett was slow to make new friends there, preferring to maintain his friendships with those who had been at Portora with him. Additionally, the majority of students taking Modern Languages was female. Beckett had previously attended single-sex establishments and, doubtless, his constitutional shyness inhibited him from forming new friendships. Once formed, however, they tended to be constant and warm.

He marked his third-year academic success by organizing his first visit to France. He travelled to Tours, hired a bicycle and set off on a tour of the châteaux and places of literary interest in the Loire Valley. He befriended a fellow tourist – an American student

Previous page *Beckett during his time as a student at Trinity College, Dublin.*

named Charles Clarke – with whom, the following year, he visited Florence and Venice, staying on there for some time to improve his spoken Italian before sitting the final Moderatorship examination at Trinity. During his final undergraduate year Rudmose-Brown put Beckett's name forward for appointment as Trinity College's exchange lecturer at the École Normale Supérieure in Paris. He did so in the expectation that Beckett would perform very well – an expectation fulfilled when Beckett came first in the college and won the gold medal in Modern Languages. Beckett was duly ratified as the college's exchange lecturer at the École. An administrative difficulty arose that prevented Beckett taking up the appointment until the autumn of the following year, 1928. But on graduation late in 1927 Beckett's future seemed reasonably secure: after completing his year in Paris (in the event he was to stay for nearly two years) it was expected that he would join the staff of Trinity College as an assistant lecturer in the French department and that a distinguished career as an academic and scholar would follow. His experience in Paris, though, would comprehensively subvert these expectations.

There was, however, nearly a full year to go before he could take up the post in Paris and the terms of his Moderatorship required him to produce a research essay. This he did by submitting an essay on a minor movement – *Unanimisme* – in modern French literature, written in the summer of 1928, no copy of which has yet come to light. He also secured, through Rudmose-Brown's influence, the position of English and French teacher at Campbell College in Belfast where he taught for the first two terms in 1928. He did not enjoy his time in Belfast, finding it dull and without culture, nor did he find formal teaching to be in any way rewarding. By far the most important event of this 'limbo year' (his phrase) was his encounter and entanglement with his first cousin, Peggy Sinclair.

Beckett's aunt, Frances (his father's only sister, known as 'Cissie'), had studied painting in Dublin and Paris and married William (known as 'Boss') Sinclair, a dealer in art and antiques. Her Beckett connections, while tolerating the marriage, did not fully approve because of Boss's 'trading' background and his Jewish origins. In the early 1920s Boss and Cissie emigrated with their children to Kassel in central Germany. Beckett had known his aunt, uncle and cousins in Dublin before their move to Germany but his family did not encourage close contact because of the Sinclairs' apparent bohemianism and disregard of conventional respectability. In the summer of 1928, when the Sinclairs were on holiday back in Dublin, Beckett met Peggy again, now an attractive, vivacious and uninhibited seventeen-year-old, and fell for her. It was not his first time in love – in his second undergraduate year he had been (along with quite a few other young men) infatuated with a fellow student, Ethna McCarthy, another vivacious and unconventional young woman. The warmth was all on his side and she did not encourage him; his feelings cooled to friendship, which they maintained intermittently until her death in 1959. Peggy was not as sophisticated as Ethna, which may have made her all the more attractive to Beckett. It did not recommend Peggy to his parents, who worried when he took her out, beyond the reach of invigilation, in a small touring car they had bought for him – he was an exuberant rather than a careful driver and was successfully prosecuted for careless driving in 1937 – and who were also worried about consanguinity. Heated rows took place in the family, further alienating Beckett from his parents. From their perspective their younger son seemed set for a bright future but he was trouble, too. Despite his parents' hostility Beckett went to Germany in the autumn of 1928 and continued his liaison with Peggy prior to going to Paris to take up his delayed appointment. He returned to Germany for the Christmas vacation and for the Easter and summer vacations of the following year, but by then the ardour of the relationship was cooling as Beckett's life took on a different complexion in Paris.

Beckett at work at the Schiller-
Theater, Berlin, in 1965. He relished
the opportunity to direct his own
plays.

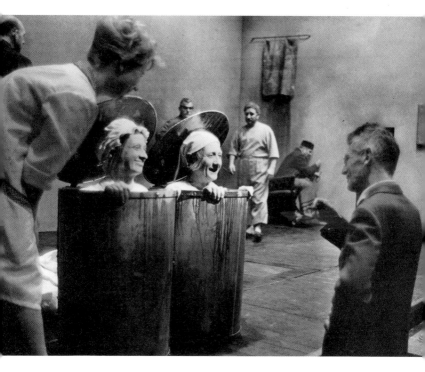

Rehearsing Endspiel *at the Schiller-Theater, Berlin, in the autumn of* 1967.

3

The École Normale Supérieure provided Beckett not only with a teaching job – with very light duties – but also with a place to stay when he arrived at the beginning of November 1928. And it gave him a new colleague and important friend in the person of Thomas MacGreevy, a native of Tarbert in County Kerry where he had been born in 1893. He had seen action as a lieutenant in the British Army during the First World War and had taken his degree in Political Science and History at Trinity College, winning a Moderatorship, as had Beckett. He was a poet, art critic and essayist, and a man of wide experience, knowledge and acquaintance. Like many Irishmen he was a fine talker but unlike many he was a sympathetic listener too. All in all, he was a godsend to someone as complicated and inexperienced as the 22-year-old Beckett. Right through the 1930s and beyond Beckett was to confide in MacGreevy as in no other, as is evident from the large collection of letters from Beckett to him, now in Trinity College. It was through MacGreevy's good offices that Beckett was to meet the two most important Irish artists then living: James Joyce and Jack Yeats.

It is not known for certain when Beckett first read Joyce's work – James Knowlson, Beckett's authorized biographer, suggests some time in the latter half of 1927 or early 1928 – but he had a letter of introduction to Joyce from Harry Sinclair (Boss's brother, who had known Joyce before he left Dublin) with him when he arrived in Paris. We may conclude, therefore, that Beckett's keenness to meet Joyce was a manifestation of his regard for the older man's work. Beckett would have had no difficulty in obtaining copies of Joyce's work as Trinity College was and is a copyright library and would have held copies of both *Dubliners* and *A Portrait of the Artist as a Young Man*. *Ulysses*,

Facing page *The Joyce family just after settling in Paris in 1920. Beckett's 'entanglement' with Lucia (seated, left) ended unhappily for both of them. Beckett's close relationship with Joyce was re-established when Beckett moved permanently to Paris in 1937.*

Beckett with Alain Robbe-Grillet,
another of the great innovators in
French prose fiction.

while banned in the United Kingdom and in Northern Ireland, was available in the Irish Free State. Harry Sinclair's letter proved unnecessary in the event, as MacGreevy brought Beckett to Joyce within a few days of the former's arrival in Paris.

Joyce was impressed by the young Beckett: by his wide reading in a number of languages; by his interest in music and philosophy; and by his high regard for the plays of J. M. Synge (1871–1909). Most of Synge's plays had remained in the repertoire of the Abbey Theatre after his early death and Beckett had attended performances of them during his time at Trinity College. (Joyce had been so impressed by Synge's *Riders to the Sea* that he translated it into Italian. He failed to secure a performance licence for that version but he did produce the original play in Zurich during the First World War.) The fact that Beckett was a fellow Dubliner may also have prejudiced Joyce in his favour. By the end of his first month in Paris Beckett was sufficiently established in the Joyce circle to be engaged or commissioned to write an essay on Joyce's *Work in Progress*, which had begun to appear piecemeal in 1924 and almost monthly in *transition* – the Paris-based literary magazine edited by Eugene Jolas – from 1927. Beckett's essay, 'Dante... Bruno. Vico.. Joyce', appeared in *transition* in June 1929 (it had already appeared a week or two earlier as one of twelve essays published in book form by Shakepeare & Company – the first publishers of *Ulysses* – under the title *Our Exagmination Round his Factification for Incamination of Work in Progress*). The same issue of the magazine also carried Beckett's first short story. His career as a writer had begun.

The double issue of *transition* (no. 16–17) in which Beckett's two pieces appeared was the one in which the editor, Jolas, announced 'the Revolution of the Word'. Jolas was of the view that Joyce was central to this revolution, dedicated to a 'complete metamorphosis of the world' through acts of aesthetic autonomy deriving from individual creativity and thus transcending ideological and religious orthodoxies. In basic terms what Jolas was calling for was the restoration to literature of the 'Orphic voice', the human voice that had once commanded nature and melted the hearts of the gods themselves. Beckett's two pieces chimed well with Jolas's editorial concerns. The polemical and provocative essay castigated Joyce's uncomprehending readers for being 'decadent' and unable to receive the 'pages and pages' of 'direct expression' provided in *Work in Progress* and made the suggestive analogy between the way Joyce was using the English language (and others) and the operations of Dante in assembling a synthetic or artifical dialect of the vulgar tongue in which to write his great epic poem. The story, 'Assumption' (reprinted only once in Beckett's lifetime), was a modest and somewhat Joycean piece in so far as it appears to dispense with plot and character in any conventional sense, though it does retain an objective narrator. What recommended it to Jolas as worthy of publication was, no doubt, its account of a young man damming up in himself some, literally, unspeakable expressive desire, which is finally released through the ministrations of a woman ('Woman', in the story) wearing 'a close-fitting hat of faded green felt'. When the release happens it rends and kills him. The final line of the story reads: 'They found her caressing his wild dead hair.' Not only the Orphic voice but Orpheus himself, dismembered by female hands. Such was Beckett's portrait of the artist as a young man.

Beckett's first appearance before the public in *transition* was as writer and critic, and it was to be some years before he decided to abandon writing criticism in favour of exclusively creative work as poet, prose writer and, later still, as a dramatist in two languages. But right through the 1930s and into the 1940s he had another, almost invisible, career as a translator of French, Italian and Spanish texts into English – invisible because many of his published translations were unsigned or uncredited. Paris in the late 1920s and early 1930s was a good place for an aspiring writer to be because numerous opportunities for publication were available, particularly for a writer who showed some promise and who was so creditably associated with Joyce and his circle. Within two years he would achieve his first separate publication with his prize-winning poem, *Whoroscope*, issued in book form in 1930 by Nancy Cunard's Hours Press in Paris; Beckett had entered the Hours Press competition for a hundred-line poem on the subject of Time at the suggestion of MacGreevy, and his winning poem was worked up in one

Nancy Cunard, publisher of Beckett's first book. Later, when she solicited artists' statements in support of the Spanish Republic, Beckett contributed the shortest one: ¡UPTHEREPUBLIC! It is not known whether she realized that this was a slogan Beckett could have read on many walls in Ireland.

night from notes he had made on the life and work of the French philosopher René Descartes. It was MacGreevy again who suggested that Beckett produce a critical monograph on the work of Marcel Proust for Dolphin Books at Chatto & Windus in London. Beckett wrote his monograph during 1930 and it was accepted and published in 1931. Chatto & Windus were to publish Beckett's series of linked short stories, *More Pricks than Kicks*, in 1934, but later, when the firm declined to publish his novel *Murphy* in 1937, he was moved to rename them Shatton & Windup.

Beckett was busy during the summer of 1930, working on his Proust monograph and collaborating with Alfred Péron – whom he had known since his undergraduate days at Trinity – on a translation into French of Joyce's *Anna Livia Plurabelle*. Life in Paris was considerably more attractive to young Beckett than life in Dublin and the value of whatever allowance he was receiving from home was increasing as sterling was devaluing more slowly than the French franc following the Wall Street Crash of the previous October. While the affair (such as it was) with his cousin Peggy had

*Rehearsing with Karl Raddatz
(Pozzo) at the Schiller-Theater in
Berlin, 1975.*

petered out at the beginning of the year, a new complication was in the making as Joyce's daughter, Lucia, became amorously disposed towards him. Since his arrival in Paris Beckett had participated wholeheartedly in Joyce's social life when invited to do so and Lucia misinterpreted his participation as interest in her. Beckett may have been less than tactful in disabusing Lucia of her notion, the result of which was that he was no longer welcome in the Joyce household on the square Robiac. Lucia was at the time experiencing the onset of a personality disorder that was to institutionalize her until her death in 1982, though it was to be well into the mid-1930s before her father would accept the irreversibility of her condition, and by then he was on easy terms with Beckett again.

Beckett delivered the typescript of his monograph on Proust to Chatto & Windus in London on his way back to Ireland in September 1930. When the academic term opened he took up his

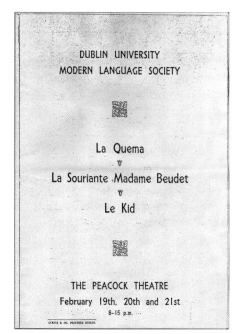

DUBLIN UNIVERSITY
MODERN LANGUAGE SOCIETY

La Quema
ʊ
La Souriante Madame Beudet
ʊ
Le Kid

THE PEACOCK THEATRE
February 19th, 20th and 21st
8–15 p.m.

The programme for the one theatrical event in which Beckett the playwright appeared on stage in public.

position as an assistant lecturer at Trinity College. Very quickly he discovered that his expectations of his students were exaggerated (a common occurrence in young academics), and that the style of teaching at university greatly differed from the one-to-one tutoring he had become accustomed to in Paris. His shyness and dislike of public-speaking compounded his problem but did not prevent him from delivering a lecture titled 'Le Concentrisme' on the fictitious French poet Jean du Chas to Trinity's Modern Language Society. Nor did it prevent him from participating in the Society's annual dramatic event at the Peacock Theatre in Dublin, where he played don Diègue in an 'entertainment' called *Le Kid* – a burlesque version of Corneille's four-act tragedy *Le Cid*. Both the lecture and the part in the burlesque suggest that Beckett was disenchanted with conventional academic life and was prepared to mock it, publicly.

Left Beckett before his first trip to Germany.

He temporarily escaped to Paris in late March 1931 to attend the launch of the French translation of Joyce's *Anna Livia Plurabelle* on which he had worked the previous summer (but which had been finalized for publication by others). While in Paris Beckett gave four poems to Samuel Putnam for his forthcoming anthology of contemporary poetry, *The European Caravan*. When published the poems were accompanied by a note written by Beckett, one of his rare autobiographical statements:

> *Samuel Beckett is one of the most interesting of the younger Irish writers. He is a graduate of Trinity College, Dublin and has lectured at the École Normale Supérieure in Paris. He has a great knowledge of Romance literature, is a friend of Rudmose-Brown and of Joyce, and has adapted the Joyce method to his poetry with original results. His impulse is lyric, but has been deepened through this influence and the influence of Proust and the historic method. He has recently won the Hours Press prize with a poem* Whoroscope, *has contributed to* transition *and* This Quarter, *and to the examination of Joyce's* Work in Progress.

This is a succinct summary of his writing career, carefully noting his

Billie Whitelaw in Footfalls *(Riverside Studios, London, 1986), the play that Beckett wrote for her in 1975.*

achievements to date (the contribution to *This Quarter* consisted of translations of three contemporary Italian poems), highlighting his work at a prestigious French school but omitting any mention of his post at Trinity College. It is clear that Beckett, even at this early stage, wished to present himself as a writer and that knowledge of his current professional status was something to suppress rather than proclaim. He was later, in 1977, to disown the poems too by not including them in his *Collected Poems in English and French*.

He returned to Dublin by way of Kassel where he was disturbed to find that Peggy's health was causing concern to her family. His own health was becoming shakier than might be expected in a young man with such an athletic history. In the late 1920s and all through the 1930s he suffered from boils and cysts, which were difficult to eradicate and which hospitalized him on at least one occasion; he experienced outbreaks of psoriasis and eczema as well. He was to pass on many of these relatively minor complaints to the characters in his post-war novellas and novels, and to supplement the catalogue of afflictions with flatulence, disorders of the feet and trouble with the joints, all calculated to image the body as a site of suffering and as a machine liable to breakdown. More worrying, however, were night sweats, tachycardia, insomnia and panic attacks, which were much more debilitating and which propelled him into psychotherapy in the mid-1930s in London. While the minor ailments may well have had their origins in poor or irregular diet or other 'lifestyle' causes, the major ones indicate the presence of stress and unhappiness. The sources of his unhappiness were several: there was his difficulty with teaching; his periodic inability to write and his impatience with the quality of what he wrote when he did succeed; and more importantly, his continuing problems at home, principally in his relationship with his mother.

The strait-laced Beckett family would have had no hesitation in countenancing a son in India because he would have been within the moral climate of the Empire. A younger son in 'gay Paree' presented a difficulty compounded by his association with James Joyce, some of whose work was banned on both sides of the Atlantic. While his letters home have not become available we may surmise that they were probably circumspect and not particularly informative as to his precise activities in Paris, or, for that matter, in Kassel. An indication of those activities, thoroughly fictionalized and deliberately obscure, is available in the novel *Dream of Fair to Middling Women* (posthumously published in 1992). James Knowlson speculates in his biography that Beckett's mother may have come across some pages of this work – written piecemeal between 1930 and 1932 – and was outraged by what she read. The most likely candidate is the story 'Sedendo et Quiesciendo' (sic) with its presentation of a 'sentimental coagulum, sir, that biggers descruption', which appeared in *transition* in March 1932 and was incorporated with some changes into the novel. Whatever the cause of her outrage the upshot was Beckett's departure from Cooldrinagh and return to his rooms at Trinity during the summer term. To find, as an aspiring writer, that what he wrote – with great difficulty – upset his mother certainly intensified his unhappiness and confirmed him in his vocational dedication. Beckett, from the outset of his career, was unswervingly committed to the integrity of his art, no matter what the personal cost in terms of his own ease or the possibilities of incomprehension by others. In this and in other areas Beckett was Joyce's most willing student.

Beckett in directorial mode in Berlin,
1965.

Tom Knight, David Warrilow and Christina Paul in a 1990 London production of Catastrophe, less than a month after Beckett's death. Beckett wrote the play in French in 1982 and dedicated it to the Czech dramatist (and now President of the Czech Republic) Vaclav Havel, who was then in prison as a dissident. Havel was elected as President of Czechoslovakia just a few days after Beckett died.

4

Unswerving commitment required full-time engagement, which could not be given while he held a post at Trinity. He went to Kassel immediately after Christmas in 1931 and it was from there that he sent his resignation to the university after the turn of the year. It was a courageous decision to terminate his employment, given that his parents had spared no expense on his education and, despite their disapproval of his behaviour, considered their younger son well placed in a secure post with fine prospects for a distinguished and respectable future. The stratagem of resigning from the distance of Germany suggests that Beckett knew his resolve to cut adrift might well have been shaken or broken had he remained at home. He may also have felt that the Sinclair family was more understanding of him and supportive of his artistic ambitions. Nevertheless, by the end of January 1932 he had left Kassel and returned to Paris to set up as a writer. From then until May he worked at his first sustained piece of fiction, *Dream of Fair to Middling Women*.

As a first novel *Dream* looks outrageously experimental, relentlessly questioning and sometimes exploding the conventions of realistic fiction. It is erudite and obscure, funny and riddling. Beckett parades his considerable learning, his close acquaintance with Romance literatures, while refusing to bow to notions of readability. What makes the novel fascinating for the contemporary reader who may be presumed to be in possession of some biographical facts, is Beckett's manner in the handling of his materials. The central character, Belacqua – described at one point as being 'a penny maneen of a low-down low-church Protestant high-brow' – offers a withering and thoroughly skewed self-portrait of the artist as a young narcissist in recoil from the business of living. The events of the novel are presented in a grotesque, almost surreal manner, calculated to impugn the tenets of realist fiction – the French realist Balzac's characters are dismissed as 'clockwork cabbages' – and Beckett's characters are gross and satirical distortions or conflations of real people. One of the principal problems with the book is its episodic structure which is slyly acknowledged by the omniscient narrator where he expresses the hope that 'the only unity in this story is, please God, an involuntary one'. That structure allowed Beckett to incorporate into the novel the story 'Sedendo and Quiesciendo' and to detach another passage for separate publication. After the book was rejected by a number of London publishers Beckett was able to salvage some of his novel by reworking parts of it and adding additional material to make the collection of linked short stories that was published as *More Pricks than Kicks* two years later in 1934.

Beckett had to leave Paris in the summer of 1932 because he did not have a valid *carte de séjour*. He was able to fund a two-month stay in London by securing an advance from an editor for a translation of Rimbaud's *Le Bateau ivre* (Beckett's translation was 'lost' for many years and did not appear in print until 1976). He tried unsuccessfully to find a publisher for his recently completed novel and for a clutch of poems; he even tried to get some book-reviewing assignments but none was forthcoming. By the end of August he was back at Cooldrinagh with no money, no job, no prospects and very little to show for his time abroad. But he buckled to, working in the garden for a small allowance, writing when he was able, translating when commissioned, reading widely, socializing a little and vigorously corresponding with MacGreevy. He was hospitalized briefly in December and again the following May for treatment for a recalcitrant cyst and for surgery to one of his feet. As he was recovering at home he learned that Peggy Sinclair had died in Germany, of tuberculosis. Within weeks Beckett's father suffered a heart attack followed by another, fatal this time, in late June. Peggy's death was a blow but the loss of his father was devastating and brought Beckett to the point of breakdown.

May Beckett's mourning for her husband was elaborate and unrelieved. The window blinds were down for months, making a gloomy Edwardian house even gloomier. Piano-playing was ruled out, and all manifestations of *joie de vivre* had to be suppressed. Nevertheless, Beckett did succeed in editing and augmenting

Beckett in the 1960s.

*Beckett at the Riverside Studios in
London in 1973.*

the unpublishable *Dream*, working at home and in the attic of his late father's offices in Clare Street, and the resulting stories were accepted in the autumn of 1933 by Chatto & Windus for publication the following year. The strain of living at home with his mother was taking its toll; the panic attacks and tachycardia returned with a vengeance. Beckett's doctor friend, Geoffrey Thompson, could find no physical problems – apart from the minor ailments – and suggested that what was needed was psychoanalysis. Such therapy was not available in Dublin so it was decided that Beckett should go to London to attend the Tavistock Clinic. The costs involved, or rather those in excess of the modest annuity allowed to him under the terms of his father's will, were to be met by his mother. The ironies implicit in this arrangement were not lost on either Beckett or his mother.

Beckett was assigned to Dr Wilfrid Bion for analysis just after Christmas in 1933 and attended regularly every week for nearly two years, with intermissions of a month or so from time to time. Progress in the therapy was slow, in pitifully small increments. Beckett's letters to MacGreevy allow an insight into Bion's therapeutic procedures, which were innovative for the time. Dream analysis, memory work and free association were all used to bring the repressed into consciousness in an attempt to come to terms with the origins and agencies of repression. Beckett's shyness and reluctance to socialize were revealed as manifestations of a deep-seated sense of superiority inculcated in him by his relatively privileged background and underpinned by his mother's high expectations of him. The fact that he had so visibly failed to measure up to her expectations caused self-loathing and pent-up frustrations, which broke out occasionally in violent temper and generalized irritability. His efforts to control or repress his feelings led inexorably to the symptoms of physical disorder that drove him into analysis in the first place. Beckett was caught in a vicious circle that took some time to break – but break it did.

His time in London was well spent in other ways too. He extended his knowledge of painting and music, formed new friendships and made contacts that brought him some reviewing and literary journalism assignments. *More Pricks than Kicks* appeared in the spring of his first year in London, to very mixed reviews and disappointing sales. Beckett was already dissatisfied with the book – which was to be banned the following year in the Irish Free State – and did not permit a new trade edition until 1970. For a writer like Beckett dissatisfaction merely propelled him into another work, in this case the novel *Murphy*, begun in 1935, finished the following year and published, after dozens of rejections, in 1938.

Murphy is Beckett's first major work of fiction and his own regard for his achievement is confirmed by the fact that soon after its publication he began translating it into French, working again with Alfred Péron (to whom he dedicated the French edition). The action of the novel is set mainly in Dublin and London and the London topography is closely related to Beckett's own familiarity with the city of his residence at the time of writing. In fact, the plight of the novel's central character, Murphy, is modelled on Beckett's own at the time, though with a greatly differing outcome. As with *Dream* the narrator here is omniscient, smart, erudite and scathing. He categorizes all the characters, except Murphy, as 'puppets', mere pieces to be moved around the board in the game played between Murphy and his stars or destiny. Again as with *Dream* the subsidiary characters are distortions, compressions or rude mechanicals standing for a range of appetites, habits or attitudes. Thus Wylie will always have his eye on the main chance; Neary will always yearn for the unattainable; Miss Carridge will never bring anything to full term; and so on. The exterior or 'big' world is a closed system governed by the rules of cause and effect, the iron laws of reciprocity. For every symptom that is eased another is intensified – humanity is a well with two buckets, one going down to be filled and another coming up to be emptied. Given such a world, or a world based on such postulates, where is individual freedom to be found? Murphy's answer is to the effect that freedom is to be found in the 'little' world, in the microcosm of the mind. Beckett issues a 'bulletin' on Murphy's mind in the shortest and most philosophically and psychologically interesting chapter of the novel, Chapter Six, but it is clear from the bulletin that Murphy is a special case, a 'seedy solipsist' more committed to exploiting how things apparently are than to understanding what they might

The final stage image from Come and Go, *written in English by Beckett in 1965 and dedicated to his publisher John Calder. The 'dramaticule' (as Beckett called it) was first played in German, first published in French and is the only Beckett play to have had its English-language world première in Dublin. This photograph is of the Gate Theatre production in 1991.*

*Beckett in London, carrying his
'pilgrim's scrip'.*

mean. The narrator describes him as 'a chronic emeritus' who lives on 'small charitable sums' – a reasonably accurate description of the author himself at the time. Murphy's fate, which he entrusts to the terms of a horoscope in which he has little faith, is to be burned to death in a gas explosion when someone pulls the wrong chain in a lavatory below his garret at the mental institution where he has found employment or, more correctly, where employment has found him. It is there that Murphy finds in the inmates a set of kindred spirits, a community of those who have withdrawn from the 'colossal fiasco' of the 'big' world to the unbreachable privacies of the 'little'.

In one reading of Beckett's presentation Murphy is a young man on the road to a 'slap-up psychosis' who is prevented from getting there by the intervention of a contingency. In this respect he is related to Beckett as a version of himself subjected to the ultimate sanction of poetic justice. While the novel may well derive some of its features from the programme of therapy undergone by the writer – he was reading widely in the available psychological literature of the time – it is necessary to bear in mind that the justice sitting in Murphy's case is Beckett and his judgement is severe. Murphy, deliberately overlooking the evident signs of anguish, envies the inmates at the Magdalen Mental Mercyseat: 'Left in peace they would have been as happy as Larry, short for Lazarus, whose raising seemed to Murphy perhaps the one occasion on which the Messiah had overstepped the mark' (Chapter Nine). The mildly blasphemous joke does not obscure Murphy's implicit death-wish, which the action of the novel fulfils just at the moment when he has begun to modify his stance towards the cleavage he perceives between the 'little' and 'big' worlds. The death of Murphy is an apposite and gruesome manifestation of what Beckett had called, in *Proust*, 'the poisonous ingenuity of Time in the science of affliction'. *Murphy* is the first extended fiction in which Beckett states and explores the themes that were to be fundamental to much of his subsequent work. These may be briefly stated as: the impossibility of achieving congruity or synchronization between the 'big' and 'little' worlds; that there is no relation between the two

*Rehearsing with Karl Raddatz
(Pozzo) at the Schiller-Theater in
Berlin, 1975.*

Billie Whitelaw in Rockaby (Riverside Studios, London, 1987), a brief play that Beckett wrote in English in 1980 and which she first played in Buffalo, New York, the following year.

systems; that the self is not unitary but serial; and that flux rather than stability is the defining characteristic of experience.

During the first phase of writing *Murphy* Beckett was asked by his friend (and sometime agent) George Reavey for a book of poems for Reavey's Europa Press. Beckett collected what he had written since the late 1920s, made a rigorous selection – dropping a few that had already appeared in print – and thoroughly revised those chosen. The collection of thirteen poems appeared under the title *Echo's Bones and Other Precipitates* in Paris in 1935. The print run for the edition was small – less than four hundred copies – and again sales were disappointing. In fact, Beckett gifted single copies of the Europa Press edition to friends and visitors right into the 1960s and included the sequence of poems in subsequently published collections of his poetry.

On one of his visits back to Dublin in 1936 Beckett finally succeeded in buying a painting from Jack Yeats (1871–1957). The painting, *Morning* (oil on canvas), cost thirty pounds and, in order to buy it, Beckett borrowed ten and undertook to pay the balance later, which he duly did. By this time Beckett had known Yeats for six years and had often visited him at the painter's studio to look at his work and for conversation. Their first meeting in 1930, like that of Beckett and Joyce two years earlier, had been effected through the good offices of Tom MacGreevy. At the time Yeats was a long-established and highly regarded artist and Beckett was doubtless in awe of him. The two had much in common despite the fact that Yeats was more than twice Beckett's age – a similar background, an interest in sport and popular forms of entertainment such as music-hall, 'varieties' and the cinema, and an abiding admiration for the work of J. M. Synge, whom Yeats had known and worked with in the first decade of the century. From Yeats's paintings (and from those of Paul Cézanne) Beckett derived the aesthetic that underpins some of the aspects of *Murphy* discussed above. Beckett responded to what he saw as the isolation and essential solitude of the figures in Yeats's paintings and was to exploit those perceptions and responses in his own work, delivering those images of the human condition that we now class under the heading 'Beckettian'.

The record of what the two men talked about is scanty, understandably so given their lifelong commitment to privacy, but it is likely that politics and the public life of the nation were discussed. Yeats, as an ardent Republican, was pleased in the spring of 1932 when the Fianna Fáil party (Republican Party) led by Eamonn De Valera surprisingly won the general election and formed a minority government with the support of the Labour Party. Yeats was probably even more pleased in January 1933 when De Valera called a snap election and won an overall majority. That election saw, for the first time – and for the next twelve years – the installation of a government composed of the losing faction in the civil war of 1922–3. Little is known of Beckett's political opinions or attitudes at the time, though there is an uncorroborated story that he 'sold' his vote in the 1933 election

The Jack Yeats painting, Morning, *that Beckett bought in the 1930s and which hung over his desk in Paris until he gifted it to the widow of a close friend.*

A break in rehearsals for Glückliche Tage (Happy Days) *at the Schiller-Theater, Berlin, in 1971.*

Working with Martin Held who played Krapp in Das letzte Band *(Krapp's Last Tape), Berlin, 1969.*

to his father for a pound. It is generally thought that MacGreevy's nationalist views influenced Beckett; they may have done but the influence can have been only marginal. In 1945 Beckett disagreed publicly with MacGreevy when reviewing his friend's monograph, *Jack B. Yeats – An Appreciation and an Interpretation* (Dublin, 1945), in the *Irish Times*. He took exception to MacGreevy's elevation of Yeats to the status of 'the national painter', pointing out that 'the national aspects of Mr Yeats's genius have, I think, been overstated, and for motives not always remarkable for their aesthetic purity', and he goes on to celebrate Yeats as one of the greats who bring light to 'the issueless predicament of existence'. He was to go further in 1954 in his own much shorter appreciation of Yeats, where he claims: 'The artist who stakes his being is from nowhere, has no kith.' By the time Beckett came to know Yeats, the painter had dropped his political enthusiasms from his paintings and had embarked on his late phase marked by exuberant handling of paint in thick impasto. Here Beckett saw, as he had seen in Joyce, 'direct expression', which he would master for himself only when he changed the language of composition of his own work from English to French. With Joyce and Yeats, Beckett found himself in the congenial company of two artists who could recruit 'the local substance' (as Beckett called it) into their work as and when appropriate but who were dedicated to getting beneath or behind it to explore the realities of being.

Beckett terminated his therapeutic sessions with Bion in the run-up to Christmas in 1935 and returned to Cooldrinagh. Over the next six months he completed *Murphy*, spent time studying Spanish and German, and forced himself to participate in Dublin's literary life. This led to him being offered the editorship of the *Dublin Magazine* but he turned it down. He entertained notions of seeking employment in an advertising agency, of training as an aircraft pilot; he even wrote to Eisenstein in Moscow asking to be taken on as a trainee cinematographer but did not get an answer. Eventually, in late September 1936, he set out on a tour of Germany. His objective was to improve his German, visit as many galleries and meet as many painters as he could.

He travelled throughout Germany for six months, touring

galleries and making contact with artists and collectors. Since his Trinity College days he had been a regular and serious

Beckett's passport photograph from the mid-1930s.

visitor to galleries and had familiarized himself with the major phases in European art. His German visit greatly enhanced his knowledge and also introduced him to some important trends in contempory art-making. He discovered that some modern paintings, classed by the German National Socialist government as 'decadent art', could not be shown or could be seen only after acquiring a special permit. He met quite a few artists (not all of them Jewish) whose work had been withdrawn from galleries or who were precluded from exhibiting at all. These experiences transformed his distaste for censorship into an implacable opposition to all institutionalized forms of it. More importantly, these experiences underpinned his antipathy to the Nazi regime, which was to find practical expression a few years later.

He arrived back in Dublin just in time for his thirty-first birthday. Again, still with no job, he had to live on the same small annuity from his father's estate as none of his publications had yet earned any royalties. The difficulties between mother and son soon re-emerged, exacerbated by the fact that he had derived no visible benefit from the trip his mother had funded. His uncle, Ross Sinclair, died in May and soon after his aunt went to South Africa with her daughters. Frank Beckett got married in August and set up home with his wife some miles away in Killiney. Beckett and his mother were left in Cooldrinagh to cope with each other as best they could. It turned out to be a poor best. Beckett's health problems flared up again and seemed as intractable as ever.

In July 1937 the Irish people approved, by a very slim majority, a new constitution for the country drafted by the Fianna Fáil government of De Valera. To someone with Beckett's libertarian views quite a few of its articles would have been objectionable or unacceptable, if not repugnant. Finally, in October 1937, he left Dublin, by way of London, for Paris, where he took up permanent residence. He had 'concurrently, simultaneously' fled and escaped. The well with two buckets mentioned in *Murphy* provides the appropriate metaphor.

5

A month later he was back in Dublin; this time as a witness for the prosecution in a libel case brought by Harry Sinclair, the late Boss's brother, against the celebrated medical practitioner and writer Oliver St John Gogarty – better known to literary history as the man on whom Joyce based his character Malachi (or Buck) Mulligan in *Ulysses*. In the course of the trial, in which Beckett featured as a witness for the plaintiff, the defence counsel did its best to discredit him by mentioning that he had written a book on the banned French writer Proust, that he had written, for limited distribution, a long poem called *Whoroscope*, and that he was the author of a banned book titled *More Pricks than Kicks*. The court was not swayed by these selected facts and Sinclair won his case with damages and costs. But the proceedings were widely reported in the newspapers and caused deep embarrassment to Beckett since his mother would have seen such publicity as sinning against her notions of respectability. During his short time in Dublin Beckett stayed with friends and did not venture to visit his mother at Cooldrinagh.

In January 1938, as Beckett and his friends the Duncans were walking home in Paris, they were approached in the street by a pimp. For no apparent reason the pimp, a man named Prudent, suddenly stabbed Beckett in the side and ran off. The blade narrowly missed Beckett's heart and lung and he soon became unconscious through loss of blood. He was rushed to hospital where it was thought his life was in danger. Within a day or two he was transferred to a private room, at the insistence of James Joyce, and made a steady recovery under the care of Joyce's personal physician. May and Frank Beckett and his wife travelled from Dublin (the winter crossing was stormy) and stayed in Paris until it was clear that Beckett would recover. During the latter part of his stay in the hospital Beckett corrected the proofs of *Murphy*, having signed a contract with Routledge before the previous Christmas. Routledge

had accepted the much-rejected novel for publication after Jack Yeats wrote a letter of recommendation, pointing out that Beckett was, on the strength of his previously published work, 'the real thing'. Joyce's concern for Beckett was manifest in the frequent visits he made and the fact that he paid the hospital bills. When the patient was discharged, Joyce wrote to Frank Beckett:

> 7 rue Edmond Valentin
> Paris 7
> 22.1.38
> Dear Mr Beckett,
> A few lines to let you know your brother has just gone back to his hotel. He is improving rapidly, has to go to the hospital in eight days for an auscultation and in [illegible word] days for a new x-ray examination, more as a precaution, I take it, than as a necessity. He will have lunch at his hotel and an early dinner at a little restaurant opposite. The Duncans will chaperon him for a time and we shall look after him too. We hope you all had a smoother passage back and are none the worse for your visit.
>   Sincerely yours,
>   James Joyce.

Beckett's relationships with Yeats and Joyce stood him in good stead while he was at a very low point in his life and career.

While in hospital he was visited by a woman some six years older than he with whom he had occasionally played tennis during his first extended stay in Paris. She was Suzanne Deschevaux-Dumesnil and within a year she and Beckett were living together and would remain so for the rest of their lives and 'legalize' their situation by marrying in 1961. Their relationship was to be and remain an 'open' one, even after the marriage, which was contracted for testamentary reasons, among others. During his long cohabitation with and subsequent marriage to Suzanne, Beckett conducted quite a number of affairs with other women, serially and severally, which to the outsider smack occasionally of French farce. Knowlson refers at one point to 'interesting

Left Beckett's mother, a life-long animal-lover, in conversation with one of her older brothers.

timetabling' as Beckett juggled with the simultaneous presence of three women in Berlin, one of them his wife.

In order to understand Beckett's apparent philandering we need to view it in a frame other than that provided by standard monogamous relationships. From *Dream* onwards Beckett's male characters feel themselves to be split, to be composed of a body and a mind; two systems not necessarily synchronized. *Murphy* memorably opens with its central character bound with scarves to a rocking-chair, the body quelled so that he can 'come alive in his mind'. At the end of the first chapter Murphy concedes that 'the part of him that he hated craved for Celia [his lover], the part that he loved shrivelled up at the thought of her'. In his novel *Molloy* the central character in the first part tells of his sexual commerce with what may have been a woman, describing their first encounter thus:

Left Peggy Guggenheim with whom Beckett had a relationship in the late 1930s. She called him 'Oblomov' (after Goncharov's character) because of his liking for staying in bed all day. He persuaded her to mount an exhibition at her London gallery for his friend Geer van Velde.

> *Poor Edith, I hastened her end perhaps. Anyway it was she who started it, in the rubbish dump, when she laid her hand upon my fly. More precisely, I was bent double over a heap of muck, in the hope of finding something to disgust me for ever with eating, when she, undertaking me from behind, thrust her stick between my legs and began to titillate my privates.*

The body has its deplorable appetites, for food and for sex, which the mind rejects as paltry. In *Molloy* there is even reference to 'the alleged joys of so-called self-abuse'. Right across the canon of Beckett's fiction there is a consistent denigration of merely physical pleasures. While it would be unwise to attribute to the writer the views of his imagined characters, it is fair to say that the consistency of such views suggests that the writer shared them, to some extent. In Beckett's relations with a number of women it appears that, after the heat of the initial amorous encounters had cooled, an *amitié amoureuse*, a loving friendship, was established, which, in some cases, endured for many years. It was as if a meeting of minds could happen only when the fussiness of the physical had been got through. Fidelity, marital or otherwise, is a redundant notion given the Beckettian view of the physical. In *Molloy* again we find: 'I would have been I think an excellent husband, incapable of wearying my wife and committing adultery only from absent-mindedness.' The body, with its pains and afflictions, its momentary pleasures, is a fatuity. Bedridden Malone is moved at one point to say: 'If I had the use of my body I would throw it out of the window.'

Having chosen to make a permanent home in Paris – he moved into a seventh-floor flat on the rue des Favorites in April 1938 (the first of only two home addresses Beckett had in Paris during the half century of his residence there), where he was joined the following year by Suzanne – it was inevitable that he should try his hand at writing in French. He may also have been motivated by his lack of visible success in his native language. Over the next two years he wrote a number of poems in French and collaborated with Alfred Péron on a translation of *Murphy*. He also rejoined the Joyce circle and widened his acquaintance with other writers and artists. The most important among these were the two van Velde brothers, Geer and Bram, both of whom were to be influential in the evolution of Beckett's aesthetics. Despite his own relative poverty Beckett bought a painting by Bram van Velde – who was even worse off – which he retained for the rest of his life, hanging it beside his writing table in both his Paris homes. At long last, at the age of thirty-two, Beckett achieved some semblance of stability in his life. It was not to last very long.

The Bram van Velde painting that impoverished Beckett bought from the practically destitute artist in the late 1930s and which hung in both his Paris apartments.

6

Beckett was in Ireland visiting his mother when war was declared on 3 September 1939. He hurried back to Paris to be with Suzanne, preferring, as he later said, 'France at war to Ireland at peace'. He and Suzanne joined the exodus from Paris in the early summer of 1940, just a few days ahead of the fall of the city to advancing German forces. They stayed briefly at Vichy, where the Joyces were also staying. It was to be the last time the two writers met, as Joyce, having succeeded in getting permission to move to neutral Switzerland, died in Zurich the following January. Beckett

Left *Beckett's mother with a pet Pomeranian. Beckett's character Molloy would later feature a similar dog in his narrative.*

and Suzanne then moved to Arcachon, on the Atlantic coast near Bordeaux, where they stayed for a few months before returning to Paris. As a citizen of the Irish Free State, neutral in the conflict, Beckett was legally entitled to remain in France. He chose to do so, but not as a neutral.

After the fall of France, Beckett's friend Alfred Péron was de-mobilized from the army; he resumed his teaching post in Paris and soon after recruited Beckett into the French Resistance. In the first phase of Beckett's Resistance activities he acted as a receiver of information collected in the field by numerous agents: this he would then collate, condense and type up in a form suitable for the preparation of microfilm to be sent to London. Beckett later dismissed this as 'boy scout's stuff' but it was dangerous work for which the French government decorated him after the war. The cell to which Beckett was attached was extensive, given the nature of its operations. The bigger the cell the greater the risk of a security breach: this eventually occurred in the autumn of 1942 and Beckett and Suzanne had to leave their flat, escaping just a couple of hours ahead of a Gestapo raid. For some weeks they were hidden in various safe houses in and near Paris and were eventually smuggled across into the Unoccupied Zone. They made their way south

Previous page The red cliffs of Roussillon in the Vaucluse, where Beckett spent some of the war years in hiding. The striking colour is remembered by one of the characters in the original French version of Waiting for Godot *but Beckett dropped the reference from his English translation.*

Right The winemaker Bonnelly is remembered in the French text of Waiting for Godot. *When he had the money Beckett bought wine from Bonnelly during the war. Local legend has it that Beckett helped with the grape harvest while he was in the Vaucluse.*

to the Vaucluse – specifically to the small village of Roussillon – where, as friends of Suzanne had intimated, residence and refuge could be arranged.

For the first few weeks they stayed at the Hotel Escoffier but soon moved to a rented house a few minutes' walk east of the village. They had very few possessions with them but Beckett had brought the growing manuscript of a novel – *Watt* (the last work he was to write in English until the mid-1950s) – which he was to complete in Paris in the early months of 1945. During the two years Beckett spent in the Vaucluse he eked out a subsistence living by working at a local farm. The agricultural work assured a reasonable supply of food, and wine was cheaply available from a local winemaker called Bonnelly, who is named in the original French text of *Waiting for Godot*. Beckett found the life dull but again he was fortunate in forming new friendships, this time with the artist Henri Hayden and his wife, Josette, and with an eccentric Irish writer named Miss Beamish, who is later mentioned under the name of Miss McGlome in the play *Krapp's Last Tape*.

The progress of the war was avidly followed by those who had access to radios and, as the Allied forces pushed north through Italy during 1943, it became increasingly obvious that the tide of war was turning. Resistance groups in Italy and France intensified their sabotage and harassment activities. Beckett voluntarily joined the local *maquis* in the spring of 1944 and became actively involved in the war effort again, but this time as a fetcher and carrier of supplies dropped by parachute in the hills of the Vaucluse. He did undergo some small-arms training but was never to have occasion to call on it. He chose not to disclose his previous Resistance efforts to his new colleagues, just as he did not tell any of his family or friends back in Dublin the following year that he had

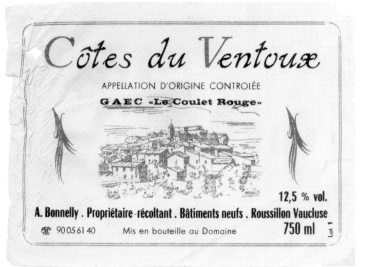

Côtes du Ventoux

APPELLATION D'ORIGINE CONTROLÉE

GAEC «Le Coulet Rouge»

12,5 % vol.

A. Bonnelly . Propriétaire-récoltant . Bâtiments neufs . Roussillon Vaucluse

☎ 90 05 61 40   Mis en bouteille au Domaine   750 ml   Lot 1

been awarded the Croix de Guerre with gold star for his work in Paris. This desire for privacy and self-effacement were to be characteristic of his behaviour for the rest of his life.

He returned to Paris in early 1945 when it became possible to do so, and set about trying to get back to Dublin to visit his family, whom he had not seen for six years. Communication with them had been difficult and sporadic due to the war. He planned to travel by way of London where he hoped to find a publisher for *Watt* and also to collect royalties on *Murphy* – his financial situation was, as ever, dire. He was to be disappointed on both counts: *Murphy* had been remaindered and the sum owed by the publisher was paltry; and *Watt* was deemed unpublishable. This was to remain the case until 1953, when it was published in Paris in the Collection Merlin by Olympia Press, though some segments of the book appeared in Irish literary journals in the early 1950s.

Right *The garden at New Place, the house close by Cooldrinagh to which Beckett's mother moved in her widowhood. It was there that Beckett began writing the novel* Molloy.

He arrived in Dublin in April 1945 and found that his mother was exhibiting the symptoms of Parkinson's disease, which was eventually to kill her in 1950. She had sold Cooldrinagh and had moved to a modest, more manageable house just across the road. It was in this house that Beckett made a two-part decision that was to alter the nature of his writing and make possible the emergence of the distinctive Beckettian 'voice' in prose fiction. Firstly, the language of composition was to be French and, secondly, the prose fictions were to take the form of first-person narratives.

In June Beckett learned of the death of Alfred Péron, who had been arrested by the Gestapo in 1942 in the sweep from which Beckett had fled. Péron had died in Switzerland a few days after the camp in which he had been held was liberated by the advancing Allied forces. The war was over but the human cost was incalculable.

Around this time Beckett discovered two further depressing facts: firstly, that the substantial balance in his annuity – which had been only partially paid during the war – could not be taken out of the country because of severe post-war currency restrictions; and,

secondly, that the provisional government in France was denying entry to all aliens, except in limited circumstances. Just as he got access to a modest capital that could sustain him as a writer he was debarred from his partner, home and place of work. His subsequent depression was compounded by the return of the physical symptoms that had afflicted him years earlier and which now forced him to consult Dr Alan Thompson (brother of Geoffrey Thompson, who had been so helpful in the past). In the course of the consultation – again, no physical bases for Beckett's apparent illness were identified – Thompson mentioned that the Irish Red Cross Society was looking for a storekeeper and interpreter to join the staff of a hospital to be constructed in the town of Saint-Lô in Normandy. This humanitarian enterprise, funded by voluntary donations and a sweepstake, finally began in August 1945 when ambulances, a lorry, some hundreds of tons of beds, medical supplies, food and equipment were shipped to Normandy.

Beckett was recruited and arrived back in France in August with the Red Cross advance party. Until January 1946 Beckett participated in the setting up of the hospital in the town, which had been almost totally destroyed by Allied bombing prior to the D-Day invasion. He arranged for the transport and storage of supplies while the hospital was being built and then for their transfer to the hospital as the buildings approached completion. He met incoming hospital staff as they arrived at various Channel ports and drove them to Saint-Lô. He was frequently in Paris on hospital business and was able to resume an approximation of normal life. By all accounts he conscientiously carried out his duties and was good company. His interpreting skills were invaluable and his command of German allowed communication with the prisoners of war who worked on the project. But by January, when his contract came to an end, he had had enough. He complained in a letter to Tom MacGreevy: 'If I don't feel myself quite free again soon, freedom will never again be any good to me.'

Right *Beckett in his Irish Red Cross uniform at Saint-Lô in Normandy in 1945. His participation in this humanitarian enterprise allowed him to return to France despite the restrictions of the provisional government.*

Above *The entrance to the Irish Hospital in Saint-Lô. Beckett wrote a short prose piece in 1946 on the significance of this enterprise. His typescript was 'lost' for many years but was eventually located in the archives of Radio Telefís Éireann and published in 1986, forty years later.*

Samuel Beckett's wartime experiences of exile and homelessness, of hunger, hardship and destitution, of destruction and devastation, were to inform nearly all the works he was subsequently to write. In an unbroadcast radio talk he wrote in June 1946 he alludes to 'this universe become provisional'. The aesthetic problem he now faced was how to use that provisionality, how to create a form to accommodate the mess and chaos characteristic not just of the post-war world but of the human condition generally. Among the many things he learned from the war was that the individual is as nothing in the face of the depersonalized forces of political ideology, the grinding forces of history itself. The town of Saint-Lô had been flattened by 'friendly fire' and had then suffered ground combat through the remains of its streets. When the surviving civilians began to filter back and commence the task of rebuilding their lives and their town, Beckett was there as a practical and involved witness. He saw that rebuilding the material fabric was a vital necessity and that continuance was not merely an option but an imperative.

7

In February 1946 Beckett was back in his Paris flat and about to undergo what he later called 'the siege in the room' and 'a frenzy of writing'. Between then and the moment he inscribed 'Fin Ussy janvier 1950' on the back flyleaf of the second manuscript notebook of *L'innommable* (*The Unnamable*) he wrote four novellas, two full-length plays and four novels as well as art criticism, poetry and translations – many of them unsigned. Curiously, the first of the novellas to be written – under the title *Suite* (later *La Fin*, translated as *The End*) – was actually begun in English but in the course of writing Beckett changed over to French to complete the story, before going back to the beginning to rewrite the entire text in French. The novella represents a breakthrough in Beckett's work, not only because of its language of composition, but also because it is cast as a first-person narrative. This narrative strategy allowed Beckett radically to alter the tonality and address of the work: gone is the pretence to omniscience of the earlier novels and stories and gone also is the 'superiority' implied in that omniscience. The first-person form allows for the construction of a fictional, subjective world at odds, for various reasons, with the social world. In *The End* the first-person narrator encounters a street-corner orator: 'He was bellowing so loud that snatches of his discourse reached my ears. Union ... brothers ... Marx ... capital ... bread and butter ...

Right *A passage from the notebook in which Beckett wrote the novella* L'Expulsé *(The Expelled) in October 1946. Note his unsuccessful attempt to write the surname Reddin backwards. At this point in the novella the narrator has been to the office of an oppressive lawyer to collect some money. He has forgotten why he received the money and the amount but he remembers the lawyer's name, which he read in reverse on a glass door at the foot of a staircase he descends while leaving the office. Beckett himself had cause to remember the name Reddin because that was the name of the judge who had found him guilty of dangerous driving arising from a traffic accident in Dublin in 1937. The conviction meant that Beckett was liable for all the legal costs and for the damage he had caused.*

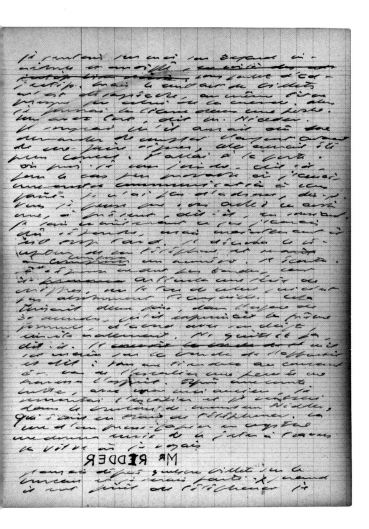

Mr RIDDER

love. It was all Greek to me.' It is evident that the narrator is linguistically skilled – he knows that an orator's speech can be classified as a 'discourse' – but he no longer subscribes to the socially determined meanings of the words in the discourse, or has decided that they have no specific relevance to him.

Having achieved this breakthrough Beckett partially drew back from it and wrote *Mercier et Camier*, a brief comic novel, which he withheld from publication in French until 1970, just after he had been awarded the Nobel Prize for Literature, and which appeared in an auto-translation into English in 1974. In the light of the four novellas and the novels of the so-called trilogy that he wrote over the next four years, *Mercier et Camier* is fairly traditional, even if it plays fast and loose with tradition by providing synopses of chapters, detailed privacies that its first-person narrator could not possibly possess, and so on. The chief importance of the novel resides in two areas: the first in its presentation of a pair of characters; and the second in the dialogue the characters have with each other. While the novel harks back to the earlier English-language work it also points forward to the dramatic work that soon followed, particularly *En attendant Godot* (*Waiting for Godot*).

By Christmas 1946 Beckett had completed the novel and the four novellas but was having little success in placing any of his work with publishers. Part of *Suite* had appeared in *Les Temps modernes* in July and a dozen poems in the November issue. His luck appeared to change in 1947 when he signed a contract with the publisher Bordas for the French translation of *Murphy* but the book sold so poorly that Bordas lost interest in publishing any more of his work. Nevertheless, Beckett kept on writing. In the first two months of the year he wrote *Eleutheria*, a play in three acts. It is a curious and uneven work, which presents as its central character a young man named Victor Krap who has withdrawn from his bourgeois Parisian family and his fiancée. It was not Beckett's first attempt at drama as he had begun and abandoned a play about Samuel Johnson under the title *Human Wishes* in the early 1940s. He had expended quite a deal of work on that abandoned play, which he later described as 'a red herring'. This first full-length play was written quickly, in just two months. It contains some

*Working with Martin Held who
played Krapp in* Das letzte Band
(Krapp's Last Tape), *Berlin, 1969.*

*Beckett in Berlin, holding a
photograph of Billie Whitelaw
in* Footfalls.

specifically autobiographical material and is audaciously conceived, using a split stage and seventeen characters. By the time any theatrical producer expressed an interest in *Eleutheria* Beckett had another play written, *En attendant Godot*, even more audaciously conceived and much cheaper to stage.

In the late spring of 1947 Beckett embarked on a novel, *Molloy*, which he thought would be the first of two but which turned out to be the first of a set of three, the trilogy of *Molloy*, *Malone meurt* and *L'innommable (Molloy, Malone Dies* and *The Unnamable)*. These novels have their origin in the novellas written earlier in that they are all first-person narratives uttered by narrators who are not accommodated to the world. *Molloy* has two narrators – Molloy himself and Moran, a private investigator who is charged with the task of finding Molloy, for reasons never made clear or explicit. In the course of Moran's pursuit he becomes more and more similar to Molloy, finding as it were a Molloy within himself. In fact, the narrator in each successive novel can be seen as an excavation to a deeper stratum of the narrator of the previous book. As each is excavated to become the next he is increasingly confined and cir-cumscribed. Molloy and Moran are both abroad in the world, hav-ing encounters and adventures. They may be uncomprehending and hampered by bodily afflictions but they are abroad neverthe-less. Malone is confined to a bed in a room and the only territory he can wander in is his imagination. The Unnamable is in an even worse situation, with neither a fixed identity nor a fixed address.

These three novels taken together constitute Beckett's major achievement as a writer. They redefine the possibilities for prose fiction in that they each dispense with plot and character as tradi-tionally conceived; the material presented in each of the narratives is subjected to relentless questioning, uncertainty and doubt; and, in the final novel, language itself is impugned as misleading and unreliable. Nevertheless, the three novels are compellingly read-able once the reader has become attuned to Beckett's concerns and methods. What sustains the reader is the prose, which can encompass effects from the most scathingly critical to the outra-geously funny, sometimes within the same sentence. Beckett's extraordinary erudition, his wide range of reference in a number of

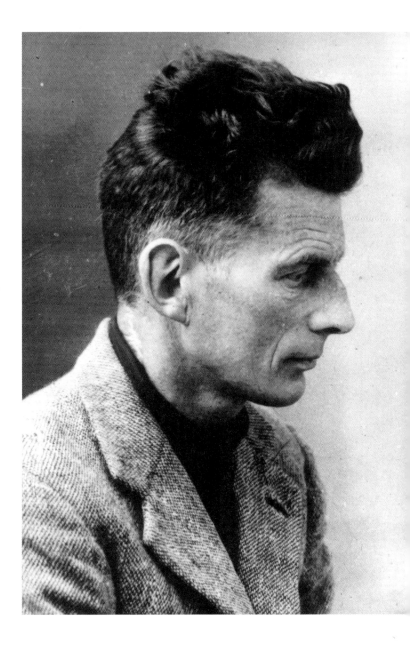

literatures, his mastery of stylistics, his precise comic timing, all are harnessed to deliver a set of novels that shock, delight, scarify and vivify.

When he had finished *Malone meurt* Beckett took a break from 'the awful prose' (his phrase) he was writing and wrote another play. He began *En attendant Godot* in October 1948 and completed the manuscript the following January. Beckett's habitual practice as a writer was to compose in longhand on the *recto* or right-hand pages of hardbound notebooks or school exercise books, keeping the left-hand *versos* free for changes to his text and, when inspiration flagged, for small doodles and cartoons, sometimes of considerable complexity. When he had finalized the manuscript he would then make a typescript version (he always did all his own typing). One of the reasons for this was practical – his handwriting was sometimes almost illegible. A work could go through numerous typescript versions before being released, though this is a feature that appears only in the latter half of his long career. In the late 1940s his practice was to make two or three carbon copies of his final typescript so as to have copies to circulate to possible publishers or theatrical directors.

Left Beckett during the late 1940s, the period of his most indefatigable creativity, when he wrote four novellas, four novels, two plays, art criticism and numerous unsigned translations.

The manuscript of *En attendant Godot* is relatively clean, indicating that Beckett composed the play with some ease. This is astounding, given that with this play Beckett rewrote the rules for the theatre, just as he had revolutionized the writing of novels by demonstrating, again and again, that what had been thought of as key elements – say plot and character – could be dispensed with as too constraining. The play is constructed on similar principles. Beckett strips away all that is inessential on the basis that a play is an event (or a non-event) that happens in a theatre in front of a live audience and that its purpose is not to have a 'meaning' but to provide an 'experience'. If the experience is sufficiently compelling to hold an audience then the audience itself will generate the meaning. The bewildering variety of interpretations of *En attendant Godot* confirms that this is indeed the case. It is further confirmed by

Beckett's practice when he came to direct his own plays from the 1960s onwards. His meticulous attention to the choreography of the movement, his rigorous insistence on the precise inflections of the voices, his refusal to engage in discussion with the actors about what a play meant, all point to a radically new, Beckettian model of theatre.

'[T]he siege in the room' lasted for nearly four years, during which Beckett and his partner had very little in the way of income. The value of Beckett's small annuity was eaten away by post-war inflation; earnings from writing were miniscule and the income that Suzanne was able to generate by dressmaking and music-teaching did not amount to very much. Nevertheless, they contrived to take holidays in a rented house at Ussy-sur-Marne, a small village about thirty miles east of Paris. Beckett found the silence of the country-side conducive to his kind of creativity and, as soon as he could afford it, in 1952, he had a modest house built there as a writer's retreat or refuge. He was able to do this with his share of his mother's lagacy after her death in 1950. He had visited his mother in Dublin each year since he had returned to France with the Irish Red Cross but in 1950 her condition deteriorated rapidly and she died, after considerable suffering, in August. Beckett was deeply affected by her death and stayed on in Dublin to settle her affairs.

Right *Beckett with a Kerry Blue at his brother's house in Killiney. Frank Beckett is in the background.*
Overleaf *The Beckett brothers relaxing in Killiney.*

But 1950 also had a more positive side for Beckett. After much hawking around of his novels and plays in typescript, first by an agent and later by Suzanne, interest in his work was awakened. Jérôme Lindon, managing director of Les Éditions de Minuit, read the typescript of *Molloy* and immediately sought to contract Beckett as a Minuit author. Disengagement from Bordas was negotiated and Minuit publication of Beckett's work began in 1951 with *Molloy* and *Malone meurt*. Minuit continues to be Beckett's exclusive publisher in France and it is a measure of Beckett's deep regard for Lindon that he nominated him as literary executor of his estate. Again in 1950 a French actor and director, Roger Blin, decided to

Above Frank's daughter, Caroline, took this photograph with her box camera of her father and uncle in the sitting-room at Shottery in Killiney.

Right Beckett with his niece, Caroline, and nephew, Edward, in the driveway at Shottery.

En attendant Godot finally realized on stage at the Théâtre de Babylone in Paris, 1953. Within a few months the play had been translated into German and was playing in Germany. It took Beckett until the end of that year to finalize his English translation of the play.

stage *En attendant Godot* but, for various reasons, mostly financial, the opening of the play did not happen until January 1953 at the Théâtre de Babylone in Paris. Minuit published the text of the play some months in advance of the first production, which had the desired effect of informing the critical debate generated by the play. Selected scenes from the play were performed on French radio in February 1952 and a message about the play from Beckett himself was also broadcast in the programme. Beckett participated in the rehearsal process at the Théâtre de Babylone, lightly changing and revising the play to suit the circumstances of the venue and the cast. It later became a hallmark of his involvement in directing his own plays that he regarded each production as offering opportunities for revisions and fine-tunings.

Beckett at work in Berlin, 1976.

Left Beckett in rehearsal for Warten auf Godot at the Schiller-Theater, Berlin, in 1974.
This is regarded by some as the definitive production of the play. The changes and revisions
Beckett introduced for this production have since been incorporated into the revised text
of his play in English. Walter Asmus, who was Beckett's assistant at the Schiller-Theater,
has directed numerous productions of the play since, most memorably for the Gate
Theatre in Dublin.

Above The author-director at work at the Schiller-Theater in Berlin.

Barry McGovern playing Vladimir in
Walter Asmus's great Waiting for
Godot *for the Gate Theatre in*
Dublin.

Stephen Brennan's Lucky at the Gate Theatre, Dublin.

Barry McGovern as Vladimir and Johnny Murphy as Estragon at the Gate Theatre, Dublin.

'All mankind is us, whether we like it or not.' McGovern and Murphy at the Gate Theatre, Dublin.

PIKE THEATRE CLUB
HERBERT LANE
OFF BAGGOT STREET

WAITING FOR
GODOT

BY
SAMUEL BECKETT

..... such terrifying and compelling intensity that 2¼ hours
.. seemed to pass in ten minutes— *Irish Times* .... we shall
certainly feel impelled to see it for ourselves— *Independent* ....
.. telling passages of highly effective writing which hold an
audience by the sheer power of their appeal— *Irish Press* ..
.. puts Dublin on the world map of drama— *Evening Mail* ..
. an attempt to out-Joyce the Joyce of "Ulysses"—*Evening Herald*

BOOKING AND MEMBERSHIP AT
BROWN THOMAS' GRAFTON ST.
PHONE 73418
OR AT THEATRE FROM 7.30 p.m.

Beckett's reputation as an important French writer was established with the publication of two novels in 1951 and consolidated by the critical reception for *Godot* in 1953. By the late spring of that year the play had already been translated into German and by autumn at least two productions were playing in Germany. A group of expatriates who ran a literary journal called *Merlin* brought out the first edition of *Watt* (completed eight years earlier) in conjunction with Olympia Press and published an English version of the first novella, *The End*. And Barney Rosset of the recently established Grove Press in New York contracted to publish all of Beckett's work, in English. Thus from the beginning of his career as a 'famous author' Beckett was confronted by the problem of translation. After a couple of collaborations with two members of the *Merlin* group Beckett decided that for him the best and only way to meet the problem was for him to translate himself.

He wrote a first version (he called it 'rushed') of *Waiting for Godot* in the summer of 1953 and revised it before the end of the year for publication by Grove Press in September 1954. Almost a full year was to pass before the play

The poster for the first Irish production of Waiting for Godot, *directed by Alan Simpson in 1956. Theatre criticism has become somewhat more sophisticated since then.*

was staged in England and Ireland, to considerable acclaim, but American audiences had to wait even longer. After the first production in London, Faber & Faber contracted to publish all of Beckett's dramatic works. His other work did not command Faber's attention: this fell to John Calder of Calder & Boyars, who became the British publishers of Beckett's non-dramatic work. Thus the play in which 'nothing happens, twice' (the late Vivian Mercier's great phrase) delivered to Beckett publishing outlets for anything he cared to release. His problem at this time was that he had written very little – the thirteen brief *Textes pour rien* (*Texts for Nothing*) – since he had finished the third novel of the trilogy in 1950, and the attention generated by *Godot* intensified the demand for translations of his recent work in French.

And then, in May 1954, came the news that his brother, Frank, was terminally ill. Beckett went to Dublin and stayed for nearly four months until after the inevitable happened. He assisted as best he

could, repeating yet again an experience he had gone through with both his parents. When he could find the time he revised the translation of *Molloy* for publication by Olympia Press and the *Merlin* group and began the translation of *Malone meurt*. In mid-September Frank died and the last link to the Cooldrinagh days was gone. The opening sentence of *Malone Dies* – 'I shall soon be quite dead at last in spite of all' – must have had a peculiar resonance for Beckett, written as it was in his dying brother's house. It is becoming increasingly clear, as research into Beckett's life continues, that his work, once thought to be impersonal, stays surprisingly close to his experience.

Left The Beckett brothers in the garden at Shottery in the summer of 1954, shortly before Frank's death.
Below The entrance to Cooldrinagh. The bullet hole in the name plaque is the result of a shooting incident in the 1980s, long after the Beckett family had moved away.

8

Godot greatly altered Beckett's life: for the first time in a writing career begun back in the early 1930s his work was yielding him a handsome income, more than enough to sustain the unostentatious lifestyle to which he had become accustomed following wartime privations and post-war austerities. The other great change was that he had unwillingly become a celebrity, with all that such status entails. His way of handling this new situation was to strictly control personal access to him by journalists and the growing band of critics and scholars who wanted to meet him. He deflected most inquiries to his publishers and stoutly defended his privacy. He quickly acquired a reputation for reclusiveness, which he did nothing to disavow. And he retreated to Ussy whenever he could, to the silence and solitude he needed for his work, and for the physical labour of gardening when the work was held up.

On returning to France after Frank's death, Beckett went to Ussy where he tried to bring into shape and expression some ideas and scenarios that he may have been working on since as early as 1952. It was to take almost two more years of much interrupted work before the new play, *Fin de partie*, was completed and another year for it to be realized on stage at the Royal Court in London, in French. Writing to the American theatre director Alan Schneider –

Right *Jean Martin, Germaine de France and Georges Adet in the first production of* Fin de partie *(Endgame) in 1957. Beckett described (in a letter to Alan Schneider) the experience of performing the play in French at the Royal Court in London as 'rather grim, like playing to mahogany, or rather teak'.*

Beckett's correspondence with whom is the only substantial body of his letters yet published – he described the new play as '[r]ather difficult and elliptic, mostly depending on the power of the text to claw, more inhuman than *Godot*'. In the period he spent working towards his final text Beckett thought long and hard about the nature of theatre and responded positively to a request from the dancer Deryk Mendel for a mime

piece. He wrote *Acte sans paroles* (*Act without Words 1*) in a matter of weeks and achieved an astonishing, wordless distillation of the central thematic concerns of *Waiting for Godot* and of the

Left *Deryk Mendel in* Acte sans paroles *(Act without Words 1) in 1957. This mime piece was requested from Beckett by the performer.*

play he was struggling to write. This short, twenty-minute mime is a signpost to the nature of the work to come – characterized by brevity, compression, distillation down to the pure drop, to what is called 'the meremost minimum' in the late prose text *Worstward Ho* (first published in 1983 and written in English).

In fact, the latter half of the 1950s, despite the 'fuss' and 'misunderstandings' (Beckett's words) caused by *Godot*, saw the relentless and indefatigable creativity of the latter part of the 1940s redeployed and redirected but this time in French and English. While working on *Fin de partie* he was also translating *Malone meurt* into English and writing a prose piece, *From an abandoned work*, which he published first in a college magazine called *Trinity News* in Dublin in 1956; and immediately after completing his French play he responded to an invitation from BBC Radio to write a play in English. *All That Fall* resulted from the invitation and the characters and setting are mainly drawn, as Beckett himself conceded, from 'boyhood memories' of Foxrock. The play is a bitter and sometimes hilarious comedy – Beckett used the word 'gruesome' to describe it – in which the paltry consolations of religious faith are found wanting given the fraught and painful nature of ordinary life.

On publication there was an immediate demand from directors and publishers for *Fin de partie* to be translated. Beckett was reluctant to undertake the effort it would require. Writing to Alan Simpson of the Pike Theatre in Dublin, who had just concluded a very successful run and a national tour with the first Irish production of *Godot*, he said: 'I do not contemplate translating the play into English for some time and indeed I feel at the moment that it is not for export at all (assuming anyone wants to import it).' He added at the end of the letter (dated 19 July 1956), 'It goes without saying that if I ever do the new play in the eye into English and if you want it it is yours in Eire or whatever the name of the place is now.' Eleven months later he finalized the translation,

Alan Stanford as Hamm and Barry McGovern as Clov in Endgame *at the Gate Theatre in Dublin. This 1990 production was directed by Antoni Libera, one of Beckett's Polish translators.*

In 1967 Beckett went to Berlin to direct Endspiel (Endgame) *at the Schiller-Theater.*

lamenting that the play lost a deal of its force in the translation process.

Beckett was a harsh judge of his own writings: on the covers of the notebooks containing the manuscripts of both *Mercier et Camier* and *Premier amour* (both written in 1946 and withheld from publication until the 1970s) Beckett inscribed the word 'jettisoned'. When the present writer asked permission to make a television adaptation of one of the stories in *More Pricks than Kicks* Beckett refused, saying 'the material is no good'. When pressed on the matter and asked if he was the best judge of his writings, his answer was monosyllabic: 'Yes.' Yet while he was translating and bemoaning what he regarded as the inevitable losses, it seems that the act of translation stimulated his creativity in the target language. Thus while he was translating *Malone meurt* into English he wrote *From an abandoned work*. Similarly, some years later, while translating the difficult *Comment c'est* into English as *How It Is*, he made the first jottings of what finally emerged as the play *Happy Days*.

His creativity responded to other kinds of stimuli as well. He heard the Irish actor Patrick Magee reading passages from *Molloy* and *From an abandoned work* on radio and on audiotape and was so taken by the quality of Magee's voice that he set about writing a play for the voice with the working title of the *Magee Monologue*. This eventually became *Krapp's Last Tape* and is probably Beckett's most accessible play and the one he most often directed himself, in English, French and German. While the sound of Magee's voice prompted Beckett to write the play, he brilliantly solved the theatrical problems inherent in staging a monologue by the simple expedient of introducing a tape-recorder, so that what the audience hears is the live Krapp on stage and the younger Krapp recorded on tape, and the drama is generated by the contrasts and discrepancies between the two versions. When Beckett wrote the play, reel-to-reel tape-recorders were relatively new to the public – during composition Beckett was driven to

Overleaf left Brenda Bruce as Winnie in the British première of Happy Days *at the Royal Court in 1962.*

Overleaf right Peggy Ashcroft in a production of Happy Days *directed by Peter Hall at the National Theatre and the Royal Court in 1974.*

Patrick Magee as Krapp in Krapp's Last Tape, *directed for BBC television by Donald McWhinnie in 1972.*

Beckett directing Krapp's Last Tape
for the Berlin stage in 1972.

requesting an instruction manual on such machines from the BBC – and so the presence on stage of a machine of this type proposed an apparent anachronism. This Beckett solved in the opening stage direction: *A late evening in the future*. Simplification of this sort was to join with his commitment to compression and brevity and to inform his writing, for various media, during the rest of his active career.

Krapp's Last Tape is a crucial text in the Beckett canon for a number of reasons, not the least being that it is a monologue, or a staged first-person narrative, and so permitted him to assimilate to or import into his writing for the theatre the restless energies that had earlier been released by his adopting a similar form in his French prose fiction of the 1940s. After *Krapp's Last Tape* he produced *Happy Days* (1961 – mostly monologue though there are two characters), *Play* (1963 – with three characters, each of whom utters a separate and interrupted monologue), *Eh Joe* (1965 – for television and using a single male mute actor and a female voice-over), *Not I* (1972 – a pure monologue), *That Time* (1975 – three intercut monologues spoken by the same voice) and *A Piece of Monologue* (1979). In each successive play the mobility of the actors is tightly circumscribed or eliminated, the scenic design is reduced and simplified so that theatre is stripped down to its primary constituents – light and voice. These plays share another common feature – they were all written in English.

Previous page left *Rosemary Harris, Robert Stephens and Billie Whitelaw in Beckett's Play at the Old Vic in 1964, directed by George Devine with Beckett's assistance. Earlier that year Beckett had assisted with a French production of Comédie in Paris.*

Previous page right *Billie Whitelaw playing Mouth in Beckett's Not I at the Royal Court in 1973.*

The bold experimentalism of Beckett's dramatic writing from 1960 onwards inevitably drew him into a more 'hands on' participation in the realizing of his texts – not only as adviser but as director as well. In London, Paris and Berlin he formed close working relationships with theatre companies and a number of actors with whom he found it particularly rewarding to work. In Stuttgart, the television company Suddeutscher Rundfunk provided him with access to the most advanced video technology then available for

Samuel Beckett at work.

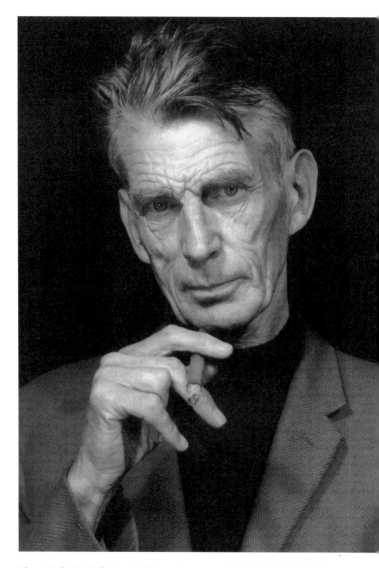

Above Beckett in Berlin in 1969, the year he was awarded the Nobel Prize for Literature.
Right The cast and crew of Warten auf Godot at the Berlin Schiller-Theater in March 1975.

Warten auf Godot"   8. März 1975

Walter D. Asmus   Hans Bogner   Klaus Herm   Horst Bollmann
Torben Seuss   Carl Raddatz   Edoardo Somma

*Beckett on the set for his television
play* Quad *in Stuttgart in May 1981.*

the making of his television plays. The price, to Beckett, of all this direct participation – 'theatre business, management of men' (in W. B. Yeats's phrase) – was a reduction in the time he was able to

Overleaf left and right *Two studies of Beckett in Stuttgart, where he directed his plays for television.*

spend at his writing-desk in Paris or Ussy. He met that apparent limitation by compressing and abbreviating the prose and poetry texts that he continued to produce, mostly in French. From this period come the numerous, brief texts that he called 'residua' and 'fizzles'. Accompanying this regular stream of new work there were the expectations of his readers and publishers for translations. The volume of proofs for checking and the necessary correspondence with three English-language publishers and one French, not to mention the work generated by occasional magazine and journal publication and his commitment to checking proofs of translations into other languages, made enormous and imperious demands on his time. At a time when most people are planning to retire or have already done so, Beckett was busier than he had ever been and his creativity – what he had memorably called 'the obligation to express' – was as fecund and flexible as ever.

That flexibility is marked by Beckett's foray into film-making. In the spring of 1963 his American publisher, Barney Rosset, invited him to write a film script. By June Beckett had completed a detailed scenario and the following summer, 1964, he went to the United States for his only visit. Beckett had written the scenario with a particular Irish actor in mind – Jack MacGowran – who in the event was not available so Buster Keaton was cast instead. The film – titled, with typical Beckettian brevity, *Film* – was shot on location and in a studio in New York, in stifling heat and humidity. By all accounts Beckett enjoyed the project, working closely with the director, Alan Schneider, and the crew. It took over a year for Beckett and Schneider to arrive at a final cut – a process lengthened by Beckett's return to France immediately after shooting had finished – but he professed himself pleased with the final product. As with the two mimes he had written in the late 1950s, *Film* is wordless throughout, except for a 'Sssh!' in the opening sequence. Again, as with the mimes, the decision to eschew words offered

Left *Beckett in Paris in 1966. At
this time his heavy involvement in
theatre led to his production of brief
and dense prose texts.*
Above *Beckett with his German
publisher, Siegfried Unseld, Stuttgart
1978.*

Above *Beckett in New York during the filming of* Film *in the summer of 1964.*
Right *On the set of* Film *in New York.*

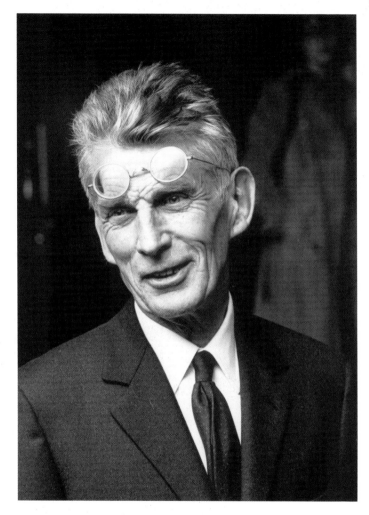

Above Beckett in May 1970, soon
after the award of the Nobel Prize.
Right Beckett signing the deluxe,
limited edition of The Lost Ones at
his Paris apartment.

Beckett an opportunity to distil or realize his thematic concerns in purely visual form without any loss of potency.

In the latter half of the 1970s and early 1980s Beckett began to scale back his work in the theatre and television and in the space that opened up he wrote three texts (novels or novellas, but they are really *sui generis*) that were considerably more expansive than anything he had written for some years. These were *Company* (1980, written in English but his translation of the text into French appeared first), *Mal vu mal dit* (1981, and published in English as *Ill Seen Ill Said* in 1982) and *Worstward Ho* (1983, written in English and judged by Beckett to be 'untranslatable', though his long-time friend Edith Fournier produced an admirable version in French, *Cap au pire*, in 1991). After *Worstward Ho* he insisted to many of his correspondents and friends that his 'writing [was] at an end'. He did so to me when we met in Paris in 1988. He quoted the final sentence of *Worstward Ho* – 'Said nohow on' – saying that he meant it literally. I countered by suggesting that if anyone possessed the know-how to go on, it was he. He demurred and I did not possess the temerity to tell him that in the briefcase at my feet under the café table was a bootleg copy of a typescript, dated July 1986 and titled 'Fragment for Barney Rosset'. This finally appeared as the tripartite prose work *Stirrings Still* (1988, translated into French and published as *Soubresauts* in 1989). The final stirrings produced yet another work, *Comment dire*, which he translated as *What is the word* in the last year of his life.

Beckett in London in 1984, his last visit.

9

Life's grip on him was tenacious and, despite the many minor afflictions that had plagued him from time to time throughout his life, his constitution was robust. In the mid-1980s, however, he had to have recourse to oxygen at regular intervals to cope with emphysema, a condition exacerbated by years of smoking. Towards the end he suffered a couple of falls that hospitalized him and then sent him to a nursing home for physiotherapy. Suzanne predeceased him in July 1989 and he was well enough to attend her funeral. Late the following month the Canadian academic Hugh Kenner (who has written a number of fine critical studies of Beckett's work) and I called on him at the cheerless nursing home on the rue Rémy-Dumoncel. Kenner and he had not met for nearly a quarter of a century and had much to discuss. The bottle of whiskey we had brought was drained during the hour that the three of us spent together. There was much smoking by all of us – Beckett was back on his favoured small cigarillos – and talk of numerological patterns in his and in Joyce's writing. Just before we left, Beckett recited, in a quavering voice, the last verse paragraph of W. B. Yeats's poem 'The Tower', a fragment from the final lines of which, ... *but the clouds* ..., he had used as a title for one of his television plays in 1976. Yeats's poem had first appeared in book form in 1928, the very year that Beckett had first arrived in Paris. It made a most moving valedictory. In December he was moved from the nursing home to hospital again and died there on the morning of 22 December. He is buried with Suzanne in Montparnasse. The grave is marked by a plain block of polished granite, inscribed with their names and dates.

The simple Beckett plot in Montparnasse.

The fact that Beckett was a bilingual writer gives rise to particular problems and opportunities for readers, critics and scholars. Anyone who reads the work in the two languages of composition quickly realizes that a text translated by Beckett himself is, in many ways, a special case. As he translated his own work from French into English, or vice versa, he was not constrained by notions of 'fidelity' to the text being translated, feeling free to alter, transpose or change as he deemed fit. What this means, of course, is that the work takes on a double existence and the only priority one can ascribe to the 'original' version is a chronological one.

The novella *Premier amour* is a case in point. Beckett wrote it in 1946 but was not satisfied with the work and put it aside. Some time later he looked over it again and wrote the word 'jettisoned' on the cover of the notebook containing the manuscript. Nevertheless, in the early 1970s Beckett released it for publication in French (the language of original composition) and translated it into English, changing and altering as he went. The resulting *First Love* is, in effect, a separate work written nearly a quarter of a century after the 'original'. The lag in time between versions can give rise to some amusing alterations. In his first post-war novella, *La Fin*, Beckett's narrator expresses his surprise that it is possible to masturbate up to the age of fifty; in the translated version, *The End*, that surprise is intensified as he realizes it is possible to perform the act up to the age of seventy. There is a gap of some fifteen years between the two versions.

The situation regarding Beckett's plays is even more complicated. His own involvement in productions of his work, as adviser and later as director, allowed him the freedom or licence to adapt his texts to the specific needs or capabilities of performers and theatrical spaces. An additional layer of complication arises from the fact that much of his direct and most satisfactory theatrical involvement took place with German companies and he 'fed back'

14e Arrt

ALLÉE
SAMUEL BECKETT

FOXROCK 1906 – PARIS 1989
ÉCRIVAIN IRLANDAIS
PRIX NOBEL DE LITTÉRATURE

The municipal authorities in Paris named a walkway off the Avenue Coty for Beckett. During the final years of his life Beckett liked to walk here as it was equally accessible from his apartment on the Boulevard St Jacques and the nursing home on the rue Rémy-Dumoncel, where he spent some months before his death.

revisions from that work into French and English versions of the plays.

Theatrical productions, however, are ephemeral by nature. When the curtain comes down the show is over and the next performance will not necessarily be an exact repeat of the previous one. Film, on the other hand, is more stable – the captured performance is 'fixed' and invariable (which may be one of the reasons why Beckett was reluctant to authorize film versions of his plays). The recent Beckett on Film Project, led by Blue Angel Films, whatever the merits or otherwise of the individual films, has opened up access to Beckett's dramatic works to a much wider and more diverse audience. The critical debate that will inevitably arise will confirm Beckett's reputation as one of the most interesting and challenging writers of the twentieth century.

Susan Fitzgerald in Footfalls, *directed by Walter Asmus at Ardmore Studios in Ireland, April 2000.*

A scene from the second act of the film version of Waiting for Godot, *shot in County Monaghan in December 2000, directed by Michael Lindsay-Hogg.*

A production still from Play, *filmed in Pinewood Studios in May 2000, directed by Anthony Minghella.*

Jeremy Irons as Listener in Ohio Impromptu, *directed by Charles Sturridge and filmed at Ardmore Studios in Ireland, June 2000.*

1906   Born in Dublin on Good Friday, 13 April.

1915   Begins formal education at Earlsfort House School in central Dublin.

1920   Enrolls at Portora Royal School, Enniskillen. Excels at sports.

1923   Enters Trinity College, Dublin University. Continues to excel at sports but discovers a great enthusiasm for learning and scholarship during second year. Specializes in Modern Languages: French and Italian.

1926   First visit to France for a summer bicycle tour of the Loire Valley.

1927   Visits Venice and Florence and seeks to improve his Italian prior to his final examinations. Graduates first in class and is awarded gold medal.

1928   Teaches for two terms in Belfast. Takes up appointment as Trinity College's exchange lecturer at the École Normale Supérieure in Paris. Meets James Joyce.

1929   First publications, a critical article and a short story, appear in *transition*, Paris.

1930   Returns to Dublin as Junior Lecturer in French at Trinity College. *Whoroscope* published in Paris. Meets Jack Yeats.

1931   Becomes increasingly disenchanted with academic life. Publication, in London, of his study, *Proust*. Leaves for Kassel, Germany, at Christmas.

1932   Resigns from post at Trinity College by letter from Germany. Moves to Paris and completes his first novel, *Dream of Fair to Middling Women*, which is rejected (and not published during his lifetime). Returns to Dublin and attempts to salvage his novel.

1933   Father dies in June. Submits recast and rewritten novel to

Chatto & Windus. Begins programme of therapeutic psychotherapy at the Tavistock Clinic, London.

1934   *More Pricks than Kicks* published in London.

1935   Embarks on second novel, *Murphy*. A collection of thirteen poems, *Echo's Bones and Other Precipitates*, published in Paris. Discontinues therapy.

1936   Returns to Dublin to finish *Murphy*. Sets off on tour of galleries, artists' studios, collectors and critics in Germany.

1937   Returns to Dublin but decides to move permanently to Paris.

1938   Beckett stabbed in a Paris street. Corrects proofs of *Murphy* while in hospital. Starts writing in French. Begins cohabitation with Suzanne Deschevaux-Dumesnil.

1939   In Dublin visiting his mother when war is declared; returns to Paris immediately.

1940   Meets Joyce for the last time at Vichy.

1941   Returns to Paris and is recruited into the French Resistance by his friend and fellow translator Alfred Péron.

1942   Escapes from Paris just ahead of a Gestapo raid when his Resistance cell is betrayed. Finds refuge with Suzanne in the village of Roussillon in the Vaucluse. Continues to work on a novel in English, begun the previous year.

1944   Roussillon liberated.

1945   Returns to Paris. Completes *Watt*. Visits Dublin to find his mother suffering from Parkinson's. Recruited by the Irish Red Cross as Interpreter and Storekeeper for the Irish Hospital in the bombed-out town of Saint-Lô, Normandy.

1946   Finishes contract with Red Cross and resumes writer's life in Paris. Writes four novellas (*The End*, *The Expelled*, *First Love* and *The Calmative*) and the novel *Mercier et Camier* in French.

1947   Writes the play *Eleutheria*. *Murphy* published in French. Begins writing *Molloy*.

1948   *Molloy* finished and *Malone meurt* written. Begins writing
        another play.

1949   *En attendant Godot* finished.

1950   Completes the novel *L'innommable*. Signs exclusive publica-
        tion contract with Les Editions de Minuit. Mother dies in
        Dublin.

1951   *Molloy* and *Malone meurt* published in Paris.

1952   *En attendant Godot* published in Paris. Beckett builds
        'writer's retreat' at Ussy, east of Paris.

1953   World première of *En attendant Godot* at Théâtre de
        Babylone, Paris. Productions of the play in Germany later
        that year. *Watt* finally published in English (in Paris).

1954   Death of brother, Frank, in Dublin. *Waiting for Godot* pub-
        lished in New York.

1955   *Waiting for Godot* played in London and Dublin. *Molloy*
        published in English. Works on *Fin de partie*.

1956   *Waiting for Godot* opens in Miami. *Malone Dies* published
        in New York. Writes *All That Fall*, his first play for radio.

1957   *All That Fall* broadcast by the BBC. *Fin de partie* published.
        Translates *L'innommable*.

1958   *The Unnamable* and *Krapp's Last Tape* published in English.

1959   Conferred with honorary degree by Trinity College, Dublin.
        Begins new novel, *Comment c'est*.

1960   *Comment c'est* completed. Works on new play in English –
        Happy Days – and moves to new apartment on the boule-
        vard Saint-Jacques.

1961   Works at translating *Comment c'est* into English and *Happy
        Days* into French. Marries Suzanne in Folkstone.

1962   Works on new stage play, *Play*; completed the following
        year.

1963   *Play* translated into German and premièred in Germany.
        Oh les beaux jours staged in France. Writes scenario for
        Film.

1964   *Play* staged in New York. Goes to New York for making of *Film*. *How It Is* published in English.

1965   Assists with productions of *Godot* in London and Berlin. Writes *Eh Joe* for television.

1966   Assists with translation of *Watt* into French. Writes a number of 'residua'.

1967   Writes *Le dépeupleur* and *Bing*. Revises the translations of two novellas, translates a third one and the thirteen *Textes pour rien* for inclusion in *No's Knife: Collected Shorter Prose, 1945–1966*.

1969   Awarded Nobel Prize for Literature.

1970   Releases *Premier amour*, *Mercier et Camier* and *Le dépeupleur* for publication in Paris. Undergoes eye surgery for cataracts.

1971   Second eye operation. Directs *Happy Days* in Berlin.

1972   Writes a new play, *Not I*. *The Lost Ones* published.

1973   *First Love* and *Not I* published.

1974   Writes new play, *That Time*. Directs *Wartung auf Godot* in Berlin.

1975   Writes and directs *Ghost Trio* for television. *Footfalls* published in London.

1976   *Pour finir encore et autres foirades* (brief texts or 'fizzles' from the 1960s) published in Paris. Two plays for television, *Ghost Trio* and . . . *but the clouds* . . ., published in English.

1977   Directs *Krapp's Last Tape* in Berlin. Writes *Company*.

1979   Writes *A Piece of Monologue* and translates *Company* into French.

1980   *Compagnie* published in Paris, followed by *Company* in London and New York. Writes *Mal vu mal dit*.

1981   Writes *Rockaby* for Billie Whitelaw and *Ohio Impromptu* for a symposium at Ohio State University. *Mal vu mal dit* published.

1982   Writes *Catastrophe* for the Avignon Festival and writes and directs *Nacht und Träume* for German television. *Ill Seen Ill Said* published. Writes *Worstward Ho* in English.

1983   *Worstward Ho* and *What Where* published.

1984   Final visit to London to assist productions of *Godot*, *Endgame* and *Krapp's Last Tape*.

1986   Writes 'Fragment for Barney Rosset', later published as *Stirrings Still*. *The Complete Dramatic Works* published in London.

1988   *Stirrings Still* published in London and New York. Writes *Comment dire* on 29 October.

1989   *What is the word* published in New York. *Soubresauts* published in Paris. Suzanne dies in July. Beckett dies in December.

PRIMARY

Publication of Beckett's work in English is currently shared by four publishers. Grove Press publishes nearly all of the work in the United States, with the exception of one play and a few of the late prose works, which were brought out under various imprints by Barney Rosset and his collaborators after Rosset's departure from Grove Press. In Britain and the Commonwealth the dramatic texts are published by Faber & Faber, and the poetry and prose fiction by John Calder. Penguin publishes Beckett's four post-war novellas. The listing below is merely indicative.

Beckett Shorts Numbers 1–12: Dramatic Works and Dialogues (London: John Calder, 1999).

Collected Poems 1930–1978 (London: John Calder, 1984).

Collected Shorter Prose 1945–1980 (London: John Calder, 1986).

The Complete Dramatic Works (London: Faber & Faber, 1986). This edition contains nearly all of Beckett's stage plays, plays for radio and television and the scenario for *Film*. The exceptions are *Eleutheria* (see below) and the dramatic fragment *Human Wishes*, which appears in *Beckett Shorts Number 2* (see above) and *Disjecta* (see below).

The Complete Short Prose 1929–1989, edited with an Introduction and Notes by S. E. Gontarski (New York: Grove Press, 1995).

Disjecta: Miscellaneous Writings and a Dramatic Fragment, edited with a Foreword by Ruby Cohn (London: John Calder, 1983).

Eleuthéria, translated from the French by Michael Brodsky (New York: Foxrock Inc., 1995).

Eleutheria, translated from the French by Barbara Wright (London: Faber & Faber, 1996).

First Love and Other Novellas, edited with an Introduction and Notes by Gerry Dukes (London: Penguin, 2000).

Molloy, Malone Dies, The Unnamable (London: Calder Publications,

1994); fourth reprint, with corrections, of the original 1959 edition.

Nohow On (London: Calder Publications, 1992); containing *Company, Ill Seen Ill Said,* and *Worstward Ho.*

The Theatrical Notebooks of Samuel Beckett, Volumes I–IV (London: Faber & Faber, 1992–9), under the general editorship of Professor James Knowlson, offer 'revised' versions of some of Beckett's dramatic texts and fascinating insights into his work as director of his own plays.

A production consortium led by Blue Angel Films has committed nineteen of Beckett's stage plays to film. A Limited Edition DVD containing the nineteen film versions may be ordered from www.beckettonfilm.com. Information on the project may be accessed at info@clarencepix.ie.

CORRESPONDENCE

No Author Better Served: The Correspondence of Samuel Beckett and Alan Schneider, edited by Maurice Harmon (Cambridge, MA, and London: Harvard University Press, 1998).

BIOGRAPHIES

Deirdre Bair, *Samuel Beckett: A Biography* (New York: Harcourt Brace Jovanovich Inc., 1978).

Anthony Cronin, *Samuel Beckett: The Last Modernist* (London: HarperCollins, 1996).

James Knowlson, *Damned to Fame: The Life of Samuel Beckett* (London: Bloomsbury, 1996).

CRITICISM

Lawrence E. Harvey, *Samuel Beckett: Poet and Critic* (Princeton, NJ: Princeton University Press, 1970). A close and detailed study of Beckett's intellectual and artistic formation. The book was written with Beckett's active assistance.

Eoin O'Brien, *The Beckett Country: Samuel Beckett's Ireland* (Dublin: The Black Cat Press in association with Faber & Faber, 1986).

Provides much information and unrivalled pictorial documentation on Beckett's background.

The three biographies listed above provide ample bibliographies of the secondary literature generated by Beckett's work. The best way to keep abreast of critical developments is to consult one of the two dedicated journals devoted to Beckett studies: *The Journal of Beckett Studies*, currently published by the Florida State University at Tallahassee; and *Samuel Beckett Today/ Aujourd'hui*, published by Editions Rodopi BV, Amsterdam and Atlanta, GA.

Every effort has been made to contact all copyright holders. The
publishers will be happy to make good in future editions any errors
or omissions brought to their attention.

PAGE

ii Samuel Beckett. (© John Minihan)

x Samuel Beckett, 1977. (© Roger Pic)

2–3 Samuel Beckett and Suzanne, Paris, 1984. (© Carlos Friere)

4 Samuel Beckett with a young relative. (Courtesy of the Samuel
Beckett Estate)

5 Birth announcement of Samuel Beckett. (Courtesy of the *Irish
Times*)

6 William Beckett. (Courtesy of the Samuel Beckett Estate)

7 Cooldrinagh (the Beckett family home), exterior. (The Irish
Picture Library)

8–9 Cooldrinagh, interior. (The Irish Picture Library)

12–13 William and May Beckett with their niece Sheila Page and her
children. (Courtesy of the Samuel Beckett Estate)

14 Samuel Beckett with his cousin Molly Roe. (Courtesy of the
Samuel Beckett Estate)

15 Samuel Beckett with his cousin Sheila Page, 1961. (Courtesy of
the Samuel Beckett Estate)

16 Samuel Beckett. (Courtesy of the Samuel Beckett Estate)

19 (above) Samuel Beckett in the junior cricket team at Portora,
1921. (The Irish Picture Library)

19 (below) Samuel Beckett with the senior rugby team at Portora,
1923. (The Irish Picture Library)

21 May Beckett. (Courtesy of the Samuel Beckett Estate)

23 Samuel Beckett. (Courtesy of the Samuel Beckett Estate)

26 Samuel Beckett at work at the Schiller-Theater,Berlin, 1965.
(Deutsches Theatermuseum)

62 Samuel Beckett's mother and uncle. (Courtesy of the Samuel Beckett Estate)

64 Peggy Guggenheim. (Telimage/© Man Ray Trust/ADAGP, Paris, and DACS, London, 2002)

67 *Untitled* by Bram van Velde. (Centre Pompidou/Photo CNAC/MNAM Dist. RMN/© ADAGP, Paris, and DACS, London, 2002)

68 Beckett's mother. (Courtesy of the Samuel Beckett Estate)

70–71 Roussillon, Vaucluse, France. (Corbis)

73 Bonnelly wine label. (Courtesy of Gerry Dukes)

75 The garden at New Place. (The Irish Picture Library)

76 Samuel Beckett, Saint-Lô, Normandy, France, 1945. (The Irish Picture Library)

78 Entrance to the Irish Hospital, Saint-Lô, Normandy, France. (The Irish Picture Library)

81 Passage from the notebook for *L'Expulsé* (*The Expelled*). (Manuscripts Collection, Harry Ransom Humanities Research Center, The University of Texas at Austin)

83 Samuel Beckett and Martin Held, Berlin, 1969. (Deutsches Theatermuseum)

84 Samuel Beckett, Berlin. (Deutsches Theatermuseum)

86 Samuel Beckett, late 1940s. (Hulton Archive)

89 Samuel Beckett. (Courtesy of the Samuel Beckett Estate)

90–91 The Beckett brothers, Killiney. (Courtesy of the Samuel Beckett Estate)

92 Samuel Beckett and his brother. (Courtesy of the Samuel Beckett Estate)

93 Samuel Beckett with his niece, Caroline, and nephew, Edward, Shottery, Killiney, Ireland. (Courtesy of the Samuel Beckett Estate)

94 *En attendant Godot* (*Waiting for Godot*), Théâtre de Babylone, Paris, 1953. (Roger Viollet)

95 Samuel Becket, Berlin, 1976. (© Anneliese Heuer/Stadtmuseum, Berlin)

96 Samuel Beckett in rehearsal for *Warten auf Godot*, Schiller-Theater, Berlin, 1974. (© Anneliese Heuer/Stadtmuseum, Berlin)